Dr Andrew Hopkins is a recognized authority on Italian architecture.
After graduating from Melbourne University and the Courtauld Institute
of Art, London, he lectured on the Italian Renaissance and Baroque at the
Mackintosh School of Architecture, Glasgow School of Art, followed by four
years as Assistant Director of the British School at Rome. In 1996 he received
the Essay Medal from the Society of Architectural Historians of Great Britain,
and has recently written the definitive book on S. Maria della Salute in Venice
(2000). In the year of the present book's publication (2002) he took up his
current post of Editor of *The Burlington Magazine*.

Thames & Hudson world of art

This famous series provides the widest available
range of illustrated books on art in all its aspects.

If you would like to receive a complete list
of titles in print please write to:

THAMES & HUDSON
181A High Holborn
London WC1V 7QX

In the United States please write to:

THAMES & HUDSON INC.
500 Fifth Avenue
New York, New York 10110

Printed in Singapore

Palazzo Farnese, Caprarola, by
Giacomo Barozzi da Vignola,
begun 1559.

Andrew Hopkins

Italian Architecture

from Michelangelo to Borromini

208 illustrations

 Thames & Hudson world of art

For Roberto, Claudia and Daniela
and in memory of Flavio and Ilaria

Acknowledgments

My thanks go to many friends who have contributed in myriad
ways, directly and indirectly, to the writing of this book:
Richard Bösel, Bruce Boucher, Donatella Calabi, Patrizia Cavazzini,
Georgia Clarke, Joseph Connors, Paul Davies, Caroline Elam,
Deborah Howard, Maria Loh, John Newman, Christina Riebesell,
John Beldon Scott, Gavin Stamp, Joachim Strupp, Patricia Waddy,
Karin Wolfe. My thanks also to the staff of the Mackintosh School
of Architecture in Glasgow where this book was conceived, and to
the staff of the British School at Rome where it was written.

First published in paperback in the United States of America in 2002 by
Thames & Hudson Inc., 500 Fifth Avenue, New York, New York 10110

thamesandhudsonusa.com

Library of Congress Catalog Card Number 2001099496
ISBN 0-500-20361-X

Map by Draughtsman Maps

Printed and bound in Singapore by C. S. Graphics

Contents

DUCHY OF
SAVOY
(PRINCIPATE
OF PIEDMONT)

DUCHY OF
MILAN

BISHOPRIC
OF TRENT

REPUBLIC
OF VENICE

• Bergamo   Vicenza   • Treviso

Brescia   Verona   Venice

• Novara   • Milan   Padua

Turin •   • Pavia   DUCHY
OF MANTUA

• Mantua

Piacenza •

Parma •   • Reggio   • Ferrara

Genoa •   DUCHY   Modena •   DUCHY
OF PARMA   OF FERRARA (until 1598)

REPUBLIC   • Bologna
OF GENOA   DUCHY OF
MODENA

REP. OF LUCCA
• Lucca   Pesaro •
Pisa •   • Florence   DUCHY OF URBINO

Leghorn   Urbino •   DALMATIA
(Livorno) •   (VENETIAN)

• Siena   • Loreto   ADRIATIC

DUCHY OF   SEA
TUSCANY   PAPAL
STATES

• Orvieto

CORSICA
(GENOA)   • Viterbo

• Tivoli
• Rome   KINGDOM
OF NAPLES
(SPANISH)

• Naples

TYRRHENIAN   Lecce •

SEA   IONIAN

SARDINIA   SEA
(SPANISH)

Palermo •   Messina

KINGDOM
OF SICILY
(SPANISH)

MEDITERRANEAN

SEA

6

Preface

Does Mannerism in architecture exist? And how useful is the term Baroque? Because of its 'ism', Mannerism has often has been considered an art-historical movement like Impressionism and Cubism, despite John Shearman's admonition to the contrary. His highly influential book was written partly to correct the theory advanced by such historians as Wittkower and Pevsner that after the High Renaissance artists of the mid-sixteenth century deliberately rejected the classical values of balance, harmony and repose and set out to shock and to introduce discord, violence and neurotic distortion. Shearman was able to show that this was not true of poetry and painting, but that left him with 'the problem of Architecture'. Mannerism is an inadequate term for characterizing the period between the Renaissance and Baroque because it recognizes only one of the many different currents that developed within sixteenth-century architecture.

As knowledge of Vitruvius and Antiquity increased, and the use of the orders became more hierarchical and codified, innovative architects such as Michelangelo and Giulio Romano deliberately departed from the norms of proportion and order then being established. This architectural licence was considered a positive achievement by the architect and writer Giorgio Vasari in his *Lives of the Artists* first published in 1550, where he praised Michelangelo's New Sacristy in Florence precisely because it broke the established rules. As Vasari saw it, this consequently liberated architects to develop their own creative responses to classicism. But although their work might be termed 'licentious', it demonstrated a profound understanding and admiration of classical architecture, and often was based on specific Antique examples.

Michelangelo, like Bramante and Raphael before him, considered the principles of classical architecture to be a system for creating space and articulating form, not a rigid set of rules to be applied blindly. Using the analogy of language (and it is no surprise that we speak of an architectural vocabulary and the language of architecture), speakers can be pompous or rhetorical, subtle or crude – they may even tell jokes, which often rely on word-play. In the same way, once the principles of classical architecture were understood, they could be used in myriad ways to achieve different effects, and one might characterize the work of architects in the sixteenth century as a celebration of the creative possibilities of that classical architectural vocabulary. In addition, just as Shakespeare's language is both recognizable as his, and distinctly different in tone between his tragedies and comedies, so too the highly recognizable personal style of Michelangelo demonstrates a remarkable variety from the sombre and serious New Sacristy to the licentious and bizarre Porta Pia.

Stylistic analysis, focusing on the orders and their application to the elevation of a building, is the principal preoccupation of many critics. But it constitutes only one element of architectural design, and I have deliberately eschewed it. Instead, more attention is paid to the plan and space of a building because they hold the key to its function and use. In the sixteenth century significant developments occurred in the design of a range of building types: palace designs accommodated changing codes of etiquette, designs for villas began to include their surroundings, church designs took account of liturgical reforms, and designs for fortifications incorporated the latest technological advances. Fortifications changed the perimeters of cities, just as urban projects dramatically changed their centres. Treatises composed by architects such as Serlio, Palladio and Vignola, provided a new theoretical and practical background for the practice of architecture. Their treatises were structured around specific subjects, such as the building type, which reflected the requirements of the patron, whether individual or institutional, who was commissioning a specific building. Largely because of this, different bodies of knowledge were built up regarding individual building types, more important than any general theory of architecture presented in a treatise.

Terms such as Mannerism and Baroque have shifted attention away from such themes and distorted our understanding of the period 1520–1630, as have architectural histories constructed in century-long slots such as 1500–1600 or 1600–1799. Begun respectively in 1519 and 1524, Michelangelo's extraordinary New Sacristy and Library at San Lorenzo in Florence seem to mark a significant change in approach to architectural design, as, at the other end of the period, do the early Roman works of Bernini and Borromini of the 1620s and 1630s. These dates can therefore be used to define the beginning and end of a specific period of architectural development.

The structure adopted in this book is a mixed one: Chapters 1 and 3 predominantly focus on specific regions or cities and their patrons and principal architects. (This parallels the structure employed in the important new surveys by Daniela Del Pesco, and Claudia Conforti and Richard Tuttle). Chapter 2, on the other hand, examines the architectural treatise, urbanism, and some major building types, and attention is focused on the development of increasingly sophisticated plans, the spatial experience of buildings, and the notable variations that patrons and their architects could achieve within the limits of an individual building type. This has inevitably produced some overlap, since buildings by the same architects occur in both Chapters 1 and 2, and Chapters 2 and 3, and may not always be where the reader expects to find them. Numerous architects, for instance, contributed to the design and building of St Peter's between 1504 and 1612, and as the most important church of Christendom it was highly influential as a model, so it is discussed in the section on Churches as a building type, rather than elsewhere. Palladio's works are scattered throughout Chapter 2 because he created innovative buildings across a wide range of types. In every case I have had to decide which context is the most meaningful for a particular building, but I have also provided page-references in the text to link the argument to relevant buildings discussed in other chapters. Within this overall structure, the chapters have been arranged in roughly chronological order, and works have been selected deliberately to provide as much coverage as possible of each of the decades between 1520 and 1630, and of Italy as a whole.

Inevitably a short survey of such an important period must omit a great deal. Many subjects mentioned only in passing, such as architectural drawings, vernacular architecture, and temporary and unbuilt projects, deserve entire books like this in their own right. In setting to work, it was the surveys of Adolfo Venturi, Wolfgang Lotz and Rudolf Wittkower that I turned to time and time again. Necessarily much of the same ground is covered, but with the benefit of much important research undertaken in the last twenty years by scholars who have written excellent books and articles on the individual architects and themes covered here. The section on Further Reading has aimed at listing the most important of these, specifically chosen for an English speaking audience. The achievements of these scholars provided the foundations upon which this book has been built.

Chapter 1:   Michelangelo and his contemporaries

Michelangelo
The most famous example of 'licentious' architecture is the vestibule (*ricetto*) of the Medici Library in Florence, one of a series of works which included the New Sacristy designed for the conventual complex of San Lorenzo by Michelangelo Buonarroti (1475–1564) upon his return from painting the Sistine Chapel ceiling in Rome, 1508–12. Although Michelangelo never considered architecture his profession, important earlier works such as Julius II's tomb of 1505 comprised much figure sculpture set within a substantial architectural framework, as did his unbuilt façade design for San Lorenzo, commissioned by Leo X Medici (1475–1521) in 1516 but abandoned by 1519. With Leo X's support, and prompted by the death in 1519 of Lorenzo de' Medici, his cousin Cardinal Giulio de' Medici (1478–1534), later Clement VII, commissioned Michelangelo to design for San Lorenzo the New Sacristy as a family mausoleum, as well as the Library complex including vestibule, reading room, and rare books room.

These were Michelangelo's first large scale architectural works, yet the New Sacristy demonstrates his complete mastery of classical architectural vocabulary, and his deliberate choice of architectural forms which violate classical norms. These contrasting approaches are evident in the grey *pietra serena* membering of the main order, and the white carrara marble employed for the door surrounds and tabernacles. On each wall, the central arched bay and entablature are recessed, flanked by two precisely carved and fluted Corinthian pilasters which, together with the broken pilasters in each corner, delimit the two narrower side bays. Michelangelo thus copied the arrangement of the south wall of the Old Sacristy by Filippo Brunelleschi (1377–1446), a system of membering in dark stone which suggested logical structural support, and which was continued in the attic zone and the pendentives below the dome. By comparison, the white marble door lintels supported by console brackets seem also to form the bases of the blind aedicules above, which are squeezed between and almost overlap the adjacent pilasters. Jarring T-shaped rectangular volumes appear to hang from the protuberant curved aedicule pediments, which look too heavy to be supported by the thin abstract pilaster strips devoid of orders. Above the tombs two sets of paired pilasters with grotesque capitals are surmounted by projecting blocks with balusters.

3

1. Only after ascending halfway up Michelangelo's extraordinary staircase (designed 1558) in the vestibule (begun 1519) of the Medici Library in San Lorenzo, Florence, can one begin to glimpse the Reading Room (begun 1524). The unorthodox triangular pediment of the monumental entrance overlaps the adjacent orders, a motif repeated elsewhere.

2, 3, 4. The plan of the monastic complex at San Lorenzo in Florence reveals the symmetry of Brunelleschi's Old Sacristy (1419) and its pendant, Michelangelo's New Sacristy (begun 1519). The separate Library sequence included the vestibule and staircase, the Reading Room, and the projected rare books room. Both the New Sacristy and the Reading Room reveal Michelangelo's sophisticated use of contrasting materials to create a highly articulated architectural framework.

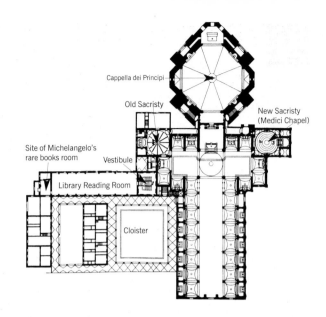

Cappella dei Principi

Old Sacristy

New Sacristy (Medici Chapel)

Site of Michelangelo's rare books room

Vestibule

Library Reading Room

Cloister

5. Ammannati executed Michelangelo's staircase design in stone rather than wood as originally planned (1559–71) thereby emphasising further its sculptural qualities. The central flight of the staircase was described by Michelangelo as a series of 'overlapping oval boxes'.

Garlanded swags decorate the space above the flanking aedicules, while a small bracket above the central bay appears to provide the only link between the marble architecture of the tombs and the architecture of the Sacristy as a whole.

After the election of Giulio as Clement VII in 1523 work began on the pendentive zone, with its extraordinary splayed windows, and the dome with antique coffering modelled on that

of the Pantheon. Simultaneously the Library project was revived 7 and after much discussion it was decided to construct the reading room as a third storey above the existing west wing of the cloister. The raised location would protect the collection from dampness and flooding and also enabled the provision of windows which faced east, following two of Vitruvius's recommendations for designing libraries as set out in his *Ten Books on Architecture.* To provide access to the reading room from the second storey of the cloister Michelangelo created a vestibule and staircase. The vestibule is relatively small, square in plan, and 1,5 has almost no space to move in except onto the extraordinary staircase that occupies its centre. The elaborate architectural articulation of the four walls was once again based on a striking colour contrast, here between the grey stone membering and the white plasterwork. The wall articulation is also startling because of its plasticity, based on multiple planes created by projecting elements and recessed volumes that would normally be associated with an exterior façade rather than interior walls. At entrance level paired console brackets seem to hang from the walls into which they are recessed, visually contradicting what ought to be their function of supporting the paired monolithic composite Doric columns of the main order. These paired columns are also recessed into the wall, behind the white plastered bays which appear to have pushed through the architectural framework, thus dissolving any perception of a principal wall plane in favour of multiple surface layers. Set into the bays are substantially projecting dark stone aedicules with deeply hollowed-out centres, surmounted by barely outlined frames with shallow recessed blind windows.

Visitors arriving at entrance level are surrounded by solid basement walls. Ascending the staircase they realize that the main storey comprises solid walls with blind aedicules articulated within a continuous framework of columns, and that the only opening is the door to the reading room. On entering, where visitors would expect to find a continuation of the columnar order 4 rising from floor level, they instead find that the main pilaster order commences above the reading room desks where it can be seen in its entirety for the length of the room. The pilasters are just one of several combined elements that establish a coherent visual framework which defines in three dimensions the entire interior space of this long rectangular volume. The pilasters on the end walls define the two side bays which the reading desks occupy, leaving only the central bay at floor level to serve as a

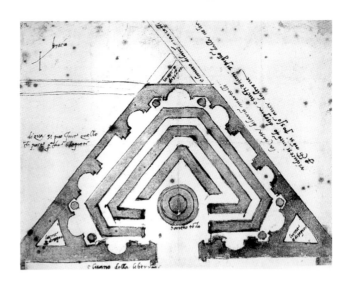

6. The rare books room for the Medici Library was never built. This autograph plan reveals Michelangelo's conception of furniture as a fundamental component of the interior space.

corridor-like passageway. The vertical lines of these pilasters continue on the ceiling, just as the pilasters of the long walls rise in line with every third reading desk to connect with the cross beams which logically and regularly divide the ceiling into a grid. Because of the location of the reading room, structural supports had to be inserted into the building below, and it was important that the new room add as little weight as possible. To achieve this the pilasters, which appear to be solely decorative, in fact form a light but strong skeletal framework which provides the structural support for the library ceiling. Michelangelo greatly reduced the wall thickness between the pilasters by ingeniously designing the bays as a succession of recessed layers which are so deeply hollowed out that the frames of the windows set into the bays do not project beyond the level of the pilasters. The visual logic of the room depended on many details of Michelangelo's design which were only completed after his departure for Rome in 1534, such as the ceramic floor tiles designed by Niccolò Tribolo (1497–1550), and the wooden ceiling and reading desks carved by Battista del Tasso (1500–55), who would also have executed the purpose-built furniture of the projected rare books room had it ever been built. This was to have been a small triangular room, located at the end of the reading room, and Michelangelo's drawing reveals his interest in complex plans, with a niche flanked by columns projected in each corner, and semi-circular and rectangular niches along each wall providing a continually varied surface. The plan is unusual also

6

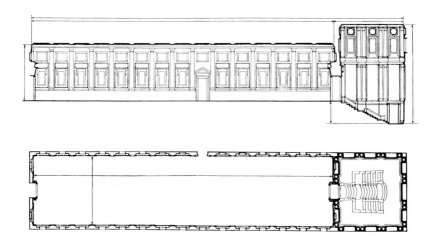

because it depicts built-in furniture, in this case the labyrinthine bookshelves, demonstrating Michelangelo's interest in every aspect of space and function.

Michelangelo's three projected spaces are usually considered in sequence from vestibule to rare books room, but it is important to consider them also in reverse order, as these spaces look different when seen from the opposite viewpoint. The reading room would have appeared even larger and more light-filled if leaving the small, windowless rare books room. The vestibule, which cannot be seen from the reading room, suddenly reappears upon arrival close to the reading room door, from where the extraordinary staircase looks quite different from when seen from below. Michelangelo had originally designed a traditional staircase consisting of flights located on the perimeter wall, but Clement VII wanted a stair that took up the whole vestibule, so Michelangelo designed one upper and three lower flights joined at a central landing. The two outer ramps have no balustrades as they were for liveried servants to stand on during the ceremonial entrance of dignitaries via the central ramp. Originally planned of walnut to match the reading room's desks, the furniture-like aspect of the staircase, which emphasized its interior location, would also have emphasized its quality as a sculptural element independent of the walls.

Much of the vestibule was executed under the supervision of Giorgio Vasari (1511–74), who eventually convinced Michelangelo in 1558 to send from Rome a small terracotta model of the staircase which was executed in stone by Bartolomeo Ammannati (1511–92). The central flight has convex oval treads divided into sets of 5, 7, and 3 steps of slightly increasing width on descent, described as resembling oozing lava, or by Michelangelo as 'overlapping oval boxes', which seem to be in danger of sliding down onto the floor. The fact that this extraordinary work was executed by Ammannati and his generation explains why Michelangelo's licentious Florentine architecture influenced them so profoundly and was adopted by them so widely. Vasari, who helped complete the Library complex, defined the crucial issues that these works had raised, when he wrote of the New Sacristy that Michelangelo 'did the ornamentation in a composite order, in a style more varied and more original than any other master, ancient or modern, has ever been able to achieve. For the beautiful cornices, capitals, bases, doors, tabernacles, and tombs were extremely novel, and in them he departed a great deal from the kind of architecture regulated by proportion, order, and rule which other artists did according to common usage and following Vitruvius and the works of antiquity but from which Michelangelo wanted to break away. The licence he allowed himself has served as a great encouragement to others to follow his example; and subsequently, we have seen, the creation of new kinds of fantastic ornamentation more of the grotesque than of rule or reason. Thus all artists are under a great and permanent obligation to Michelangelo, seeing that he broke the bonds and chains that had previously confined them to the creation of traditional forms'.

Vasari understood the importance of Michelangelo's Florentine work for the subsequent development of sixteenth-century architecture. Vasari also set out a vision of historical development that is still current today: the influential Roman works of Donato Bramante (1443–1514), in particular the Cortile del Belvedere and the Tempietto, gave impetus to a normative architectural vocabulary of High Renaissance classicism, including an accepted way of disposing of the orders and creating space, that became established in the period leading up to Michelangelo's departure from Rome in 1516. Michelangelo, who had worked in the Vatican side by side with Raphael (1483–1520), and whose career culminated with his work at St Peter's – discussed separately in Chapter 2 (pp. 94–95) – was influenced by his Villa Madama begun in 1518 for Giulio de' Medici, the same patron who commissioned the New Sacristy at San Lorenzo in 1519. The architecture of the New Sacristy demonstrates perfectly Michelangelo's understanding of convention and how he chose instead to innovate through licence. Michelangelo was not the only architect who deliberately exceeded the accepted norms of architectural vocabulary, which were quickly coalescing into a formalized and orthodox canon. But because Michelangelo was the most influential artist of the first half of the century, and celebrated as such by Vasari, the startling examples of licentious architecture which he designed were enormously influential, and provided the impetus for other architects to experiment with their own creative interpretations of classicizing architecture.

Michelangelo's contemporaries

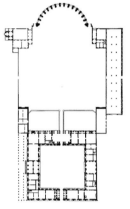

Giulio Romano (1499–1546) was contemporaneously experimenting with the licentious possibilities of classical architecture at the Palazzo Te. After training in Rome with Raphael and working on the Villa Madama, in 1524 Giulio was persuaded by the writer Baldassare Castiglione (1478–1529) to accept a commission from Federico II Gonzaga (1500–40) of Mantua to design and build a suburban villa, misleadingly called the Palazzo Te. Set on the site of some Gonzaga stables which were incorporated into the ambitious project, the four wings surrounding the courtyard have centrally located loggias that serve as entrances from the garden and outlying buildings and that provide access to each of the four L-shaped sequences of apartments. The external, internal and garden façades

10. Giulio's painted decoration for the sequence of interiors at the Palazzo Te includes the Sala dei Cavalli, where horses are represented standing on top of door lintels and pedestals, and in front of a painted architectural framework of pilasters. The fireplace was also designed by Giulio and continues the theme of oversize keystones.

each have different elevational treatments, including that of the famous courtyard where triglyphs in the frieze appear to have slipped down below the architrave, and the oversize rusticated keystones protrude below the top of the arched entrance. This deliberate architectural licence, which was Giulio's method of responding to the irregularities of the existing building, was noted with approval by the sculptor and violent libertine Benvenuto Cellini (1500–71), Vasari, and Sebastiano Serlio (1475–1554) who published a careful estimation of Giulio's achievement in 1537, 'It was the habit of the ancient Romans to mix the rustic style not only with the Doric but also with the Ionic and the Corinthian orders ... and Giulio Romano has taken more delight in this mixture than anyone else, witness various palaces in Rome and also in Mantua, that most beautiful Palazzo del Te, not far outside that city, truly a model of architecture and painting'. Serlio justified his own practice in the *Libro Extraordinario* of 1551, 'I have indulged in these licences, frequently breaking an architrave or a frieze, or the cornice, but always relying here on the authority of some Roman buildings'.

Licence with architectural vocabulary provided novelty and variety, exemplified by the rusticated façade of Giulio's own house (1540–44), and the extraordinary barley-sugar columns which seem to float unsupported on the first floor façade of the Estivale courtyard in the Ducal Palace of Mantua (1538–39). Giulio's novel application of the classical architectural vocabulary was not always simply for its own sake, and in the case of his restoration of San Benedetto at Polirone (1540–46) and Mantua cathedral (1544–46), it also enabled him to make sensitive additions to older buildings. At the Palazzo Te, Giulio created a variety of contrasting architectural settings including the garden loggia, with its sober piers and columns supporting the *all'antica* decoration of the barrel vault, that represents the perfect balance of structure and ornament first pioneered at the Vatican Loggias by the triumvirate of Raphael, and his assistants Giovanni da Udine (1487–1564) and Giulio.

The sequence of painted interiors at Palazzo Te subverts the traditional boundaries between architecture, sculpture and painting through its powerful *trompe-l'oeil* effects – remarked upon by William Shakespeare in *The Winter's Tale*, 'That rare Italian Master, Iulio Romano, who (had he himselfe Eternitie,

11

11. The Estivale courtyard of the Ducal Palace at Mantua (1538–9), represents Giulio's work at its most 'mannerist', with barley-sugar columns that seem to be merely attached as decoration to the *piano nobile* of the façade.

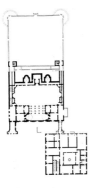

and could put Breath into his Worke) would beguile Nature of her Custome, so perfectly is he her Ape'. The decorative themes of the interior, from the Room of the Horses to that of the Giants, indicate an aesthetic which is at once playful, sensual and fantastic. The particular themes of each room were no doubt personally approved by the patron Federico Gonzaga after thorough discussion with Giulio, just as he would have purchased Gulio's series of pornographic drawings of lovemaking positions (*I modi*) as they were engraved and accompanied by the ribald sonnets of Pietro Aretino (1492–1556).

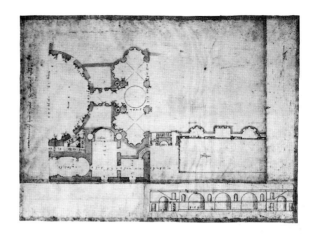

12, 13. For Francesco Maria I della Rovere and his wife, Girolamo Genga designed a large villa, linked to a smaller, earlier villa, in the hills overlooking Pesaro (begun c. 1530). The courtyard of the Villa Imperiale has balustraded and pavilioned roofs and a hanging garden. It was inspired by Raphael's incomplete Villa Madama (begun 1518).

14. Andrea Palladio was also inspired by Raphael's Villa Madama which he drew when in Rome in 1541 along with ancient buildings including the Roman baths. This fragment of a villa was an influential model for many projects in the sixteenth century, and provided continuing inspiration for architects throughout subsequent centuries.

A quite different but equally persuasive direction for classically inspired architecture was represented by the Villa Imperiale, built from around 1530 by Girolamo Genga (1476–1551) outside Pesaro in the Marches. Duke Francesco Maria I della Rovere of Urbino (1490–1538) and his wife Eleonora Gonzaga wanted their villa to emulate and rival Raphael's Villa Madama. They hired Genga as ducal architect   14 because of his training with Raphael, and on the recommendation of the writer Cardinal Pietro Bembo (1470–1547): 'Genga is a great and rare architect'. This was important testimony for a literary minded patron such as Della Rovere who had requested from Castiglione a copy of the famous letter to Leo X which Castiglione had co-authored with Raphael, that was to serve as a preface to a collection of drawings of Roman Antiquities; here the significance of these buildings and of Vitruvius was set out, as was the difference between these and good modern architecture as represented by Bramante.

The Villa Imperiale was built into a rising hill which Genga's   12, 13 design deliberately exploited to create a series of three enclosed courtyards and terraced gardens supported by fortress-like walls. The massive brick construction recalls Bramante's Cortile del Belvedere in the Vatican, and the deep apsidal niches of the entrance façade and courtyard seem carved out of the solid mass of the wall, as does the cavernous triple-arched barrel-vaulted loggia with *all'antica* coffering. Highly finished brick-work is employed for the orders and other details which articulate the building elevations, with stonework restricted to the pilaster capitals. The bronze lettering for the romanizing inscriptions on the frieze were composed by Bembo, who

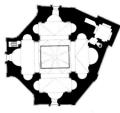

15, 16. The simple exterior of Giovanni Battista da Lucano's Sanctuary of the Madonna di Macereto (1528–38) near Visso belies its monumentality and the interest of its interior spaces. This pilgrimage church is located high in the mountains of the Marches.

described the villa as being 'designed according to the true principles of art, and with more ancient elements'. The grandiose conception of the villa's innovative sunken court was the direct precedent for that subsequently designed at the Villa Giulia in Rome. Genga's classically inspired use of brick was also evident in the façade of San Giovanni Battista in Pesaro begun in 1543 and completed by Genga's son Bartolomeo (1518–58), who was military architect to Guidobaldo II della Rovere (1514–74) and famed for his many fortifications.

A comparison of the plans of San Giovanni and the Sanctuary of the Madonna di Macereto built 1528–38 near Visso in the 15, 16 Monti Sibillini of the Marches, reveals a similar incipient recreation of antique spatial form through the use of apsidal niches in the four perimeter chapels. The Swiss born Giovanni Battista da Lucano (d. 1539) designed a powerful polygonal volume composed of austere, unadorned ashlar masonry blocks forming massive walls, out of which the four arms of the Greek-cross interior seem to be carved. The miraculous statue of the Madonna was installed in a small 'house' under the octagonal cupola in the centre of the church so that pilgrims could process around the interior, accessible via three entrances, a common

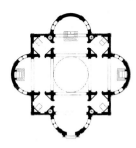

17, 18. Gianfrancesco Zaccagni designed the Madonna della Steccata in Parma on a centralizing Greek-cross plan (1521). The fine brickwork exterior comprises apses that project beyond the central square plan, defined by the four corner chapels enclosing the arms of the cross and providing structural support. Sangallo recommended providing three entrances to the church but this was not done.

19. For the Madonna di Campagna at Piacenza (1522) Alessio Tramello employed piers for the four corners of the crossing, succeeded by four small domes in the corners of the square central block of the building. Subsequent alterations included the addition of an extended chancel housing the high altar.

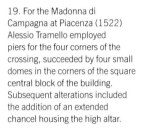

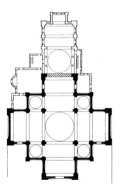

feature of many pilgrimage churches including the Madonna di San Biagio near Montepulciano designed in 1518. These sorts of functional requirements were clearly understood by architects such as Antonio da Sangallo the Younger (1484–1546), hereafter simply called Sangallo, who provided specific criticism of another important pilgrimage church, the Madonna della 17, 18 Steccata in Parma, designed in 1521 by Gianfrancesco Zaccagni (1491–1543) and initially constructed by him and his mastermason father Bernardino (c. 1460–c. 1530). This church was built to house a miraculous image of the Madonna, but the Zaccagni were sacked in 1525 and the first item in Sangallo's list of critical remarks written in 1526, was the need to provide an entrance to each of the three apses because it was a devotional church in which the whole city would need to be accommodated. Thus the theoretical purity of the Greek-cross plan with four equal arms extending from the centre ought to be modified for logistical purposes, bringing it closer in function to other contemporary pilgrimage churches such as Visso and the Madonna di Campagna at Piacenza designed in 1522 by Alessio Tramello 19 (c. 1470–1528). The exterior of the Steccata is built up in stages from the perimeter half-domes of the apses and adjacent scrolls

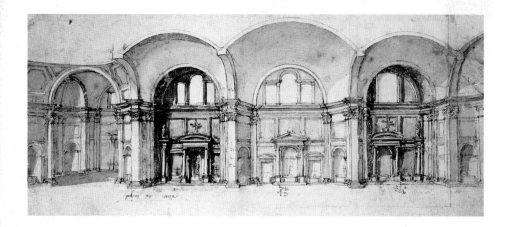

20. Baldassare Peruzzi's longitudinal section for his proposed rebuilding of San Domenico in Siena (after 1531) includes three soaring vaulted nave spaces lit by a variety of 'Serlian' and 'thermal' windows located above the monumental aedicules of the chapel altars.

21. The double-storey courtyard loggia for the Palazzo Massimo delle Colonne in Rome (1532) reveals Peruzzi's monumental conception of space, in which he introduced specific concepts derived from ancient buildings, such as the rectangular mezzanine openings that light the vault of the ground floor loggia.

to the balustrade which defines the ends of the Greek cross, and finally to the diminutive dome which surmounts only the relatively small width of the central crossing. The sparse and widely spaced articulation of the exterior pilasters at the Steccata contrasts both with the fuller interior treatment and with the new direction indicated by Michelangelo in his unrealized façade project for San Lorenzo in Florence, taken up by the Roman trained Cola dell'Amatrice (*c.* 1480–after 1547) in his design of 1525 for the lower façade of the church of San Bernadino in Aquila in the Abruzzo.

One of the architects most inspired by Bramante and Raphael's recreation of antique spatial volumes was Baldassare Peruzzi (1481–1536), who designed the Villa Farnesina (1509–11) and became joint chief architect with Sangallo of St Peter's in 1520. Peruzzi was briefly imprisoned during the Sack of Rome by the agents of the Habsburg Emperor Charles V (reigned 1519–1556), before returning to his native Siena where he was appointed chief architect responsible for fortifications, including the bastioned city gates. One of Peruzzi's most archaeologically inspired projects was his masterful proposal for the rebuilding of San Domenico in Siena after 1531. The drawing reveals Peruzzi's status as one of the greatest architectural draughtsmen of the first half of the sixteenth century, and also indicates his knowledge of ancient Roman structures such as bath complexes with their enormous vaults. Yet Peruzzi's flexibility and inventiveness in tackling difficult problems and sites meant that he often took an independent and indeed critical attitude towards Vitruvius and the antique. This was revealed in his various design proposals for St Peter's, and in the designs for the

20

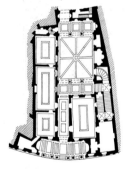

22, 23. Peruzzi's curved façade of the Palazzo Massimo includes different types of fenestration for each storey. The entrance to the palace appears to be centrally located but camouflages the asymmetrical ground plan, with the courtyard entered from a corner.

24. The Well of San Patrizio at Orvieto (1527–37) was a collaborative effort led by Antonio da Sangallo, assisted by Giambattista da Cortona and Simone Mosca.

Roman palace of Pietro Massimo, his last and greatest commission. The palace was located on a substantial curve of the via Papalis, so Peruzzi curved the rusticated façade of the building to follow the line of the street. He emphasized this feature by locating the colonnaded ground floor loggia at the central focal point of the palace. The central entrance to the loggia also established the longitudinal axis through the palace that traverses the side rather than the centre of the courtyard. Peruzzi then brought into play other axes that established the visitor's itinerary via the staircase that leads to the sequence of rooms on the piano nobile of the palace. A great sense of axiality and coherent sequential order is achieved, despite the irregularity of the site.

By comparison, Sangallo, who designed the Palazzo Farnese in Rome in 1514, represented rigid Vitruvianism, even criticizing Raphael's plan of St Peter's. Sangallo's numerous commissions were derived from his position of power as architect of St Peter's from 1520 onwards, and include the Zecca (1525–27), and fortifications in Rome, Florence, Ancona and Perugia. Sangallo's most interesting and unusual work, which demonstrated his technical capabilities without being burdened by a rigid interpretation of the orders, was the enormous Well he constructed at Orvieto, commissioned in 1527 by Cardinal

Alessandro Farnese (1468–1549), later Paul III, during his exodus from the Sack of Rome.

Sangallo's humanistic erudition was a product of the remarkable combination of papal patronage and the brilliant milieu of the Accademia della Virtù, a group including artists and architects dedicated to humanist studies. So too, in north-eastern Italy an equally flourishing humanist and antiquarian culture thrived in the circles associated with the university of Padua, where in the 1540s Andrea Moroni (d. 1560) designed the fine central courtyard of its headquarters at the Palazzo del Bò and established the first Botanical Garden in Europe. Living and working within this learned circle was the remarkable architect Giovanni Falconetto (1468–1535) who, after many years in Rome and his native Verona, moved to Padua in the early 1520s, gaining official appointment as municipal architect in 1524. In the same year the humanist writer Alvise Cornaro (1484–1566) commissioned for the grounds of his house a Loggia and Odeum, 25, 26 which were to house respectively theatrical and musical performances. Falconetto's designs were closely based on ancient Roman models but also inspired by recent architecture in Rome such as the Villa Madama, while his subsequent commission from Cornaro for the Villa dei Vescovi at Luvigliano in 1535 enabled him to design a monumental villa that was influential on the next generation of architects working in the Veneto.

27. Michele Sanmicheli's richly decorated façade for the Palazzo Bevilacqua in Verona (c. 1530) reflected the ambitions of his clients, expressed here through elaborately fluted columns set on tall pedestals framing large arched windows with victories in the spandrels. The elegant balustraded balcony clearly distinguishes the *piano nobile* from the rusticated ground floor.

28. To convey the function of the Porta Palio (begun c.1547) as one of Verona's defensive city gates, Sanmicheli employed the robust Doric order in pairs framing the entrances, surmounted by a ponderous entablature and projecting cornice. The central entrance has enormous rusticated keystone blocks untamed by the orders.

North-eastern Italy

A triumvirate of architects practising in the Veneto, Michele Sanmicheli (1484–1559), Jacopo Sansovino (1486–1570) and Andrea Palladio (1508–80), each created works displaying a remarkable variety of classically inspired architecture, partly because of their response to different building types, and partly as a response to different patrons, their requirements and status. Sanmicheli, who trained and practised in Rome and Orvieto, in 1526 accompanied Sangallo's commission for Clement VII to inspect fortifications in the papal states. Sanmicheli then settled in his native Verona where he was commissioned to design a number of palaces that demonstrate his ability to combine the language of the Roman High Renaissance with the local Veneto dialect of palace typology. A comparison of the Canossa, Bevilacqua and Lavezola palaces, all begun in the early 1530s, reveals Sanmicheli's inventive planning in relation to site and the variety of his elevational treatments.

Both the Canossa and Lavezola palaces broadly conform to the traditional tripartite palace plan used in Venice and the Veneto comprising a narrow front on a deep block. Sequences of

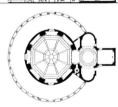

29. Sanmicheli's unusual design for the pilgrimage church of the Madonna di Campagna just outside Verona (1559) included a tall, cylinder-like central domed space with a smaller subsidiary space housing the high altar. Even more unusual is the low circular portico surrounding the rotonda.

rooms are arranged lengthwise on both floors along either side of the longitudinal axis, from entrance, to central hall, to a courtyard situated towards the rear. The sober rusticated ground floor façades surmounted by austere orders on the piano nobile can be read as representing the social status of the patrons as solid members of the Veronese patriciate. By comparison, the medieval complex of Palazzo Bevilacqua was transformed by replacing the existing forecourt with an internal ground floor loggia and long hall on the piano nobile set behind a lavish façade, of which only seven of the planned fifteen bays were built. The flamboyant Palazzo Bevilacqua, with its twisted fluted columns and wealth of ornamentation on the piano nobile, well represented the ambitions of the two brothers who lived there, Antonio and Gregorio Bevilacqua who were imperial Counts. The remarkable differences between the three palace façades, all designed in the space of a few years, indicates how significant the site and the requirements of the patron could be for the architect when determining design.

By comparison, fortifications usually had little or no architectural decoration because of their predominantly functional purpose. But Sanmicheli, inspired by Falconetto's classicizing city gates of Padua, designed the magnificent Porta Nuova (1531–40) and the Porta Palio (1547) at Verona. Their respective articulation differs. The first, in which rustication dominates, well expressed the role of a functioning bastion. The second, in which pairs of giant fluted Doric columns predominate over the

27

28

33

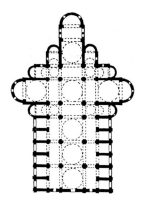

30, 31. Andrea Moroni's plan for Santa Giustina in Padua (1532) established an influential model for Northern Italian Benedictine churches. The church was built largely by Andrea della Valle who executed the clearly articulated interior including the interior piers with Ionic pilasters set above pedestals.

rustication, stated its function as a city gate with three entrances in its bold triumphal-arch façade. These works were executed by Sanmicheli in his role as military architect for the Venetian Republic, and were inspired by his tours of duty to the Venetian dominions in the Aegean where he obtained first-hand knowledge of Greek architecture, a unique distinction among sixteenth-century Italian architects.

Sanmicheli also designed the innovative pilgrimage church of the Madonna di Campagna on the outskirts of Verona in 1559, where he reconciled the theoretical and aesthetic desire for a centralized building with the practical liturgical requirements for a church with a longitudinal axis, created by the addition of a sanctuary. The tall drum-like interior accommodated religious processions, and the external porch protected visiting pilgrims from the elements, but the combination of diverse elements resulted in an odd exterior elevation. For individual projects

29

34. (Overleaf) The façade of Sansovino's Mint in Venice (1536) expresses particularly well the fortified nature of the building. The Doric columns of the first floor are heavily rusticated and the massive lintels above the windows seem squeezed between the columns and look as though they might collapse on anyone trying to enter the building through a window. The third storey was added later (1560s).

32, 33. The interior of Jacopo Sansovino's church of San Francesco della Vigna in Venice (begun 1534) was clearly articulated with dark stone contrasting with the whitewashed walls. The chancel and choir are almost equal in length to the nave of the church.

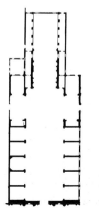

such as a pilgrimage church, the architect often had considerable freedom of design – quite the opposite of conditions that normally prevailed in ecclesiastical patronage, where religious orders had specific needs and employed traditional architectural typologies. For example, Moroni's designs for the rebuilding of the mother church of the Cassinese order, Santa Giustina of 30, 31 Padua, rendered the essence of the Veneto-Byzantine church type by surrounding the tall dome over the central crossing with three large and four subsidiary domes in the transepts, chancel, and corners of the crossing. The enormous scale of the church was also dictated by the Order's traditions and comprised a long nave, two aisles, and many side chapels, together with a complex crossing comprising two projecting transepts and a long choir to the east, which accommodated the conventuals with their specific devotional and liturgical needs.

The Franciscan order had a strong tradition of church architecture, but the impetus for rebuilding San Francesco della 32, 33 Vigna in Venice came from Doge Andrea Gritti (1455–1538) who appointed Sansovino in 1534, just as he had been instrumental in gaining Sansovino the post of architectural

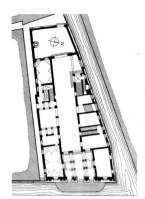

35. The plan of Sanmicheli's Palazzo Grimani in Venice (1556) ingeniously conceals the asymmetry of the site by maintaining the traditional Venetian central hallway, entered from a corner of the Romanizing entrance portico following Peruzzi's example at the Palazzo Massimo in Rome.

36, 37. Sansovino introduced a large, square Romanizing courtyard towards the rear of the Palazzo Corner in Venice (begun c. 1545). The regular fenestration across the length of the two piani nobili largely conceals the presence of the traditional Venetian hallway that traverses the middle of the palace

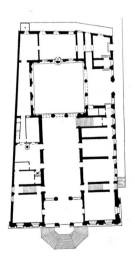

superintendant to the Procurators of Saint Mark's in 1529. When the proportions of Sansovino's plan were called into question, Gritti sought the advice of a resident Franciscan friar, Francesco Zorzi, author of the 1525 treatise on the *Harmonies of the Universe*. Zorzi recommended a series of proportions for the church plan related to musical harmonies, perceptively noting that 'one could increase the measures and numbers, but they should always remain in the same ratios ... all the measurements of the plan, lengths as well as widths, will be in perfect consonance, and will necessarily delight those who contemplate them'. The church was constructed to Sansovino's revised plans, but he suffered further interference and much greater ignominy when the principal patron, Giovanni Grimani, Patriarch of Aquileia, chose Palladio to design the façade in 1565, considering Sansovino's design of 1534 outdated.

Ironically, Sansovino had enjoyed Grimani patronage in Venice from his arrival, as Cardinal Marino, the Patriarch of Aquileia, and his brother Vettor Grimani, had helped the Florentine gain his official appointment in 1529. It was in his official capacity, and at Doge Gritti's request, that Sansovino instigated the project of urban renewal in Piazza San Marco with projects for the Mint, Loggetta, and Library – discussed in Chapter 2, Public buildings (pp. 84–85). These brought to the heart of Venice the robust romanizing High Renaissance architecture that Sansovino had already pioneered at the Scuola della Misericordia in Venice of 1532. The rusticated façade of the Mint clearly articulated a building designed as a stronghold for making and storing the Republic's currency. Sansovino provided practical stone-vaulted rooms, which were unusual in Venice, but much less a fire hazard that the traditional wooden beamed ceilings. The foundries were located at the front of the building and the rooms used for minting were arranged at the rear of the central courtyard, but the utilitarian nature of the building was belied by the presence of a grandiose double staircase located on the east-west axis, revealing Sansovino's incorporation of grander elements from palace typology.

Sansovino's subtle use of architectural vocabulary to express function and status is also evident in the application of rustication to the ground floor and mezzanine of the Palazzo Corner where it implies impenetrability, appropriate for the entrance hall and storage rooms of a palace. For the two upper floors, which contained the public reception rooms, Sansovino employed a series of paired columns which extend across the

38, 39. The Palazzo Thiene in Vicenza was probably designed by Giulio Romano (1542) and modified in construction by Andrea Palladio (1546) but left unfinished (1558). Set around a large central courtyard, many aspects of the palace are indebted to Giulio's Palazzo Te, including the abundant surface decoration of the exterior that greatly contrasts with the traditional sobriety of earlier palaces and villas in the Veneto.

entire façade and which frame each arched window. The traditional tripartite division of the Venetian palace into central hall and flanking side rooms is maintained, but only expressed in undertones by the three central windows of the two upper floors which are slightly wider than those that flank them. At the rear of the building Sansovino abandoned the tripartite division by inserting a grandiose romanizing courtyard to create a dignified space for those using the land entrance, and enabling more light to enter the rooms there. The irregularity of the left-hand side of the palace remained imperceptible because of the axiality and symmetry of the interior public spaces. The same effect was achieved by Sanmicheli at the Palazzo Grimani designed in 1556 where the sharply decreasing width from front to rear of the right hand side is not readily apparent inside the palace.

The restrictions and irregularities of many sites were often deliberately ignored by patrons who instead commissioned larger, idealizing projects in the hope that adjacent land would be acquired eventually and the entire project completed. Such was the case of the Vicentine palace for Marcantonio and Adriano Thiene begun in 1542 and probably designed originally by

35

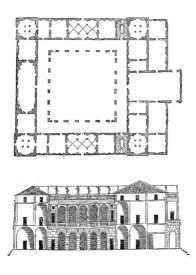

40

40. The simple, almost rustic appearance of Palladio's first villa, built for Girolamo de' Godi at Lonedo (1537–42), belies its sophisticated interior planning. The exterior has no orders and stone was employed sparingly for the staircase, the balustrades, and the window surrounds. Palladio designed villas that were economical to build and this was one of the keys to his success.

Giulio Romano and revised in execution by Palladio. The scheme envisaged an enormous arcaded central courtyard surrounded by the four wings of the palace with rooms in enfilade on the piano nobile. The axial arrangement of the interior spaces reveals a knowlegde of Roman planning, especially of bath buildings, and like the Palazzo Te included large, medium, and small rooms for different functions and for different seasons. These ideas were greatly developed by Palladio who later experimented extensively with the various sizes of rooms, their relative size in relation to each other, and the overall size of buildings, all of which were also governed by a system of proportions. Less than a quarter of Palazzo Thiene was actually built, but the monumental rusticated façade dominates the street, and the vaulted atrium with freestanding rusticated Tuscan columns conjured up the grandeur of ancient Rome.

38, 39

In the 1540s Palladio was at the beginning of his career, having returned from a visit to Rome in 1541 made with his mentor, Count Giangiorgio Trissino, who had given him the poetical nickname Palladio. Earlier, from 1524 to 1537, Palladio was a member of the prestigious Pedemuro workshop that had worked on Trissino's villa at Cricoli on the outskirts of Vicenza, built in the new Roman style in the 1530s. So too, Palladio's first villa, for Girolamo de' Godi of 1537–42, includes a central arcaded loggia, articulated without stonework or the orders, and also dominated by and subordinated to the unadorned style of the local vernacular typology. By comparison, the effect of his trip to Rome and

40

the influence of Giulio Romano can be assessed by comparing these early works with the Palazzo Thiene of 1542 where Palladio demonstrated his reconciliation of the vernacular forms of the Veneto with *all'antica* planning and style to present a miraculous synthesis that was both flexible and appropriate to the site. Palladio also achieved grandiose effects at little expense, the precise subject that his second significant patron, Alvise Cornaro, would write about in the treatise he composed in the 1550s on the practical and functional aspects of architecture.

Palladio subsequently developed much richer and complex plans and a more articulated use of the orders. At the Villa Pisani at Bagnolo of 1542 he created a cruciform *salone* based on ancient Roman baths, and he employed the orders in more elaborately articulated schema. The pedimented portico also made its first appearance, subsequently developed at the Villa Cornaro at Piombino Dese begun in 1551 for Giorgio Cornaro, and from there to the entire legacy of Palladianism. Palladio's numerous palaces and villas demonstrate his greatest achievement – the perfect understanding of the principles of classical architecture combined with the ability to go beyond established norms, enabling him to generate a different response to each situation and context. His palaces, for example, reveal a simple, stripped-down and almost abstract application of the classical orders that was the result of his formative training and practice in Padua and Vicenza. This was the main difference between his work and that of Sanmicheli and Sansovino who came north already inspired by ancient and modern Rome. Palladio's visit to Rome in 1541 with Trissino, and separate visits in 1545, 1546–47, 1549 and again in 1554 when he returned, probably with his other significant patron Daniele Barbaro (1514–70), were experiences so profound that they changed his ideas about architecture, and ushered into the north a different conception of romanizing architecture. Palladio's work encompassed all aspects of architecture and theory and are described in more detail in Chapter 2 (pp. 117, 121, 134).

Papal Rome

In 1519 Sansovino was commissioned by Leo X, in preference to his better known peers including Raphael, Peruzzi and Sangallo, to design a new church dedicated to San Giovanni on the via Giulia for the Florentine community in Rome. Although Sansovino was trained as a sculptor and had little experience as an architect, the commission was not odd because families such

41. Antonio Labacco's engraved plan and elevation (1558) record Antonio da Sangallo's proposal (c. 1520) for San Giovanni dei Fiorentini in Rome. Inspired by the Pantheon, the vast coffered and domed interior space was to be surrounded at ground level by numerous small chapels with openings set between columns on tall pedestals. The exterior was enriched at drum level with over-lifesize figurative sculpture set before large scrolls.

as the Medici had well-established networks of artistic patronage in their native city from which they preferred to select artists, in order to surround themselves with trusted allies, a common phenomenon especially of popes and cardinals in Rome. In 1518 the Florentine Giovanni de' Gaddi also commissioned his Roman palace from Sansovino, but at San Giovanni, Sansovino was unable to lay proper foundations on the sandy subsoil of the site, and Sangallo had to be called in to provide the technical expertise required. Sangallo's own proposal demonstrates the subordination of functional planning to the recreation of a Pantheon-like interior elevation. The centralized space, although theoretically preferable to architects, has no discernable axis from entrance to altar and the entrances to the numerous small chapels are squeezed between tall pedestals. Sangallo's invention of the striking volutes and over life-size figure sculpture that surround the drum became well known through its publication in 1558 among the series of architectural plates with commentary by Antonio Labacco (1495–1567).

When Leo X died in 1521 the San Giovanni project was abandoned, and other important projects in Rome were brought to a halt abruptly with the Sack of 1527. Renewed impetus only came from Paul III, elected in 1534, whose patronage extended throughout the papal states, where he commissioned works such as the Perugian fortification known as the Rocca Paolina in 1540. As a Cardinal, Paul had commissioned Sangallo to design the Palazzo Farnese in 1514, and on his elevation he had the projected palace enlarged and integrated into a wider urban scheme related to the Campo dei Fiori area of the Campus Martius. Paul oversaw the 1536 entry of Charles V into Rome, and built on the

41

42. Michelangelo's innovative plan for San Giovanni dei Fiorentini (1559) in Rome envisaged eight subsidiary interior spaces that seem to be carved out of the surrounding wall mass. This dynamic conception of interior space adumbrates many aspects of Baroque church planning.

work of Clement VII who had established the third leg of the trident of streets which emanated from the Piazza del Popolo. He improved the via del Babuino and the via del Corso, and linked them with the new via dei Condotti which connected the Piazza di Spagna with the Ponte and Castel Sant'Angelo. Throughout his papacy Paul III continued to patronise Sangallo, who worked in the Vatican Palace in the 1540s building the Sala Regia and the Pauline Chapel, as well as presenting a proposal for the completion of St Peter's. Other architects, such as Nanni di Baccio Bigio (*c.* 1507–68) and Jacopo Meleghino (*c.* 1480–1549) were employed by Paul III to design his palace on the Aracoeli hill 1535–44, adjacent to the Campidoglio where the pope had Michelangelo relocate the equestrian statue of Marcus Aurelius as part of a larger scheme to redesign the square 1539–64, and where Michelangelo created a triumphant, public Roman architecture for the Palazzo dei Conservatori. Paul III instigated the Council of Trent in 1545 to reform the structure and practice of the church, and he appointed Michelangelo in 1546 to resolve the design of the most important church in Christendom: St Peter's (see pp. 94–97).

Michelangelo had returned to Rome in 1534, after the death

of Clement VII, to be with Tommaso de' Cavalieri (*c.* 1509–87), the young nobleman he had fallen in love with. Alongside his work for Paul III, Michelangelo received commissions from his Florentine patrons including Grand Duke Cosimo I de' Medici (1519–74), who in 1559 revived the project to build San Giovanni dei Fiorentini. Several plans by Michelangelo for a centralized church survive. Two initial designs were based on an overlapping circle and square with strongly accentuated cross-axes, and an octagon with powerful diagonal axes and prominently protruding apsidal chapels. A third design demonstrated a development and resolution of Michelangelo's thinking whereby the cross-axes and diagonal axes counterbalance each other and the rectangular protrusions appropriately contain the entrances located on the cross-axes, while the chapels are enclosed within the body of the building. The two earlier designs featured structural supports in the form of thin walls, piers and columns, while in the third design spaces such as the chapels and passageways seem to be carved out of the massive masonry block

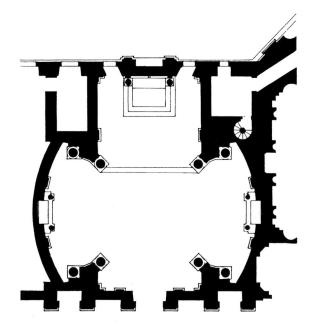

43. Michelangelo's Sforza Chapel at Santa Maria Maggiore in Rome (1561–73) is the most unconventional space built in the sixteenth century.

44. The splayed window in the vault is just one of the unusual elements of Michelangelo's Sforza Chapel at Santa Maria Maggiore in Rome (1561–73).

in the form of a square with rounded corners. Michelangelo reworked this third design to relocate the eight pairs of columns against the perimeter of the central rotonda, increasing the sense of a great vaulted space like the Pantheon which has no freestanding internal structural support. The sequence of differentiated spaces, from the apsidal barrel-vaulted entrance vestibules, to enormous central rotonda, to small elliptical chapels, is reminiscent of ancient Roman baths, although made more dynamic by the axial corridors of space which appear in plan like meteorites shooting out from an exploded sun.

By comparison, for the Sforza Chapel at Santa Maria Maggiore designed in 1561, Michelangelo created a radically dynamic space by canting diagonally in towards the centre the four columns which support the partial balloon vault of this burial chapel. The strategic placement of these four columns raised on pedestals also enabled the definition of the five interpenetrat-

43, 44

ing spaces of the central crossing, abbreviated entrance vestibule, chancel with altar, and the two butterfly-wing flanking niches which house the Sforza tombs. The curved segments which define the niche walls are so shallow that the vaults above them are less than quarter spheres, and the supporting columns for the semicircular arches of the flanking vaults seem trapped, almost hidden in the corners of the niches. The powerful forms employed by Michelangelo in this space make it seem much larger than it is, and the unorthodox arrangement of architectural elements results in spatial forms which are as difficult to describe as they are to comprehend even after long periods of intense contemplation.

The unique forms of Michelangelo's Sforza chapel represent a break with the architecture of the first half of the sixteenth century, but they also represented a difficult path that was only taken up and developed in the next century by Francesco Borromini (1599–1667). Instead, the innovative but more easily comprehended forms created by Giacomo Barozzi da Vignola (1507–1573) were more immediately influential. Commissioned by Julius III del Monte (1487–1555) in 1550, the small church of

45. At Sant' Andrea in via Flaminia in Rome (1550–53) Vignola set an oval dome over the rectangular body of this small church. Except for the façade executed in dark grey stone, the plain brick exterior is sparsely articulated.

Sant' Andrea in via Flaminia has a rectangular plan, oriented along the axis from entrance to altar which is housed in a small projecting chapel lit by two small lateral windows. The pedimented façade appears as a separate entity in grey stone applied to the lower portion of the simple box-like brick structure, which in turn is surmounted by a squat elliptical cylinder and capped by a shallow Pantheon-style dome. The rectangular interior is articulated with Corinthian pilasters, above which arches and pendentives rise to support the first oval dome to be employed in church design. Vignola successfully combined the axial direction of a longitudinal space with the sensation of centrality exuded by the dome. In 1565 he extended this exploration of spatial form by designing an entire oval interior and dome for Sant' Anna dei Palafrenieri, encased within a rectangular exterior, and executed with the help of his son Giacinto (*c.* 1534–*c.* 1584). Vignola's major works in church and villa design – the Gesù and Caprarola – are discussed in Chapter 2 (pp. 100 and 124).

Upon election in 1559 Pius IV de' Medici of Milan (1499–1565) turned to Michelangelo, as had his immediate predecessors. The task in hand was the transformation of the *tepidarium* of the Baths of Diocletian into the church of Santa Maria degli Angeli, to initiate a strategy of conspicuous ecclesiastical triumph over pagan antiquity that would be elaborated by successive popes. Pius also embarked on projects of urban improvement, enlarging, regularizing, and renaming the stretch of road between the Quirinale Palace and the Porta Nomentana as the via Pia, and replacing the old city gate with Michelangelo's striking creation. The Porta Pia (1561–64), executed with the help of his regular assistant Giacomo del Duca (1520–1604), is Michelangelo's most unusual work. The deliberate contrast between the vertical fluting of the entrance pilasters and the adjacent horizontal lines of the rustication jar visually, as does the enclosure of a large inscribed block within the triangular pediment above the gate where it appears to be supported by the insubstantial garland which hangs between the scrolled terminations of the curved segmental pediments. Although large in scale, the numerous individual elements of the doorway and framing aedicule seem small, and their composition deliberately eccentric.

In contrast to Michelangelo's Sforza Chapel, the best known work of Pirro Ligorio (1513–1583) employed to great effect shallow surface decoration. Born into a noble Neapolitan family, Ligorio arrived in Rome in 1534 and immersed himself

46. Michelangelo's Roman city gate, the Porta Pia (1561–64), included a novel entrance portal facing the city, composed of large, seemingly oversized architectural elements including the curved segmental pediments linked by a garland. A comparison with Sanmicheli's city gates reveals how wilful and personal Michelangelo's architectural style became in his later years.

in the study of its antiquities, and in 1548 became a member
of the group of artists called the Virtuosi al Pantheon. Ligorio
published his researches on antiquity in the 1550s and 1560s,
and these experiences formed the basis of his archaeological
architectural style, evident in the small Casino commissioned for 47, 48
the grounds of the Vatican in 1558 by the Neapolitan Paul IV
Carafa (1476–1559). Ligorio based his design on the model of a
Roman garden house, with a dining loggia and gateways set
around an oval court and central fountain. The beautiful stuccowork and painted decoration were based on antique motifs
executed at the instigation of Pius IV, after whom the casino is
now named, with its fountain below the loggia that was a deliberate antiquarian reconstruction of a classical Lymphaeum under
the patronage of the muses.

Apart from the grounds of the Vatican, the pope, his cardinals
and their retinues were able to take refuge in their suburban
Roman villas, and during the summer months they retired to
various villas outside Rome, a practice known as *villegiatura*. For

47, 48. For the Casino of Pius IV
(1558–65) set in the grounds
of the Vatican palace, Pirro Ligorio
created a series of vaulted rooms
decorated *all'antica*, and also
covered the exterior with
elaborately detailed stucco
decoration and statuary. The
entrances to the courtyard are
at the narrow ends of the oval,
so that the approach to the Casino,
set on one of the long sides of an
oval courtyard, is oblique.

49. Pirro Ligorio's conception for the Villa d'Este at Tivoli (1550) focused on the pre-eminence of the garden in relation to the villa, which functioned as a belvedere for splendid views out across the extensive gardens and fountains built later (1559–72) and the countryside beyond, as recorded in Etienne Dupérac's engraving (1573).

example, in 1550 Cardinal Ippolito d'Este of Ferrara commissioned Ligorio, by then his personal archaeologist, to transform an existing monastery he had acquired at Tivoli, following the successful excavation of Hadrian's Villa that Este had undertaken in 1549 with Girolamo da Carpi (1501–56). Ligorio shifted the focus from the existing building to the surrounding gardens and spectacular fountains he created, inspired by the adjacent ancient villa which was also the source for the antique statues acquired and displayed in the garden. Given this success, Pius IV

49

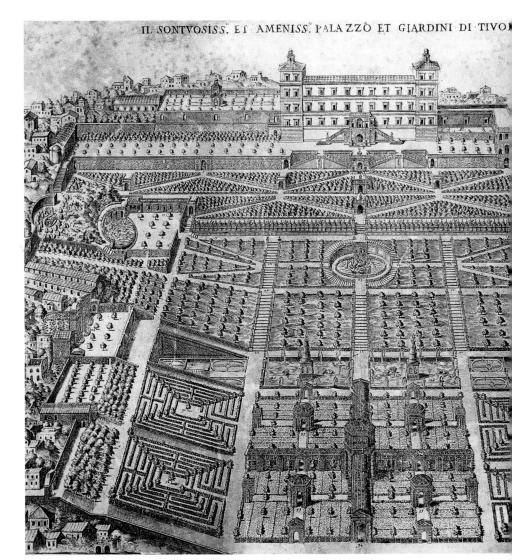

IL SONTVOSISS. ET AMENISS. PALAZZO ET GIARDINI DI TIVOI

Joannes Dominicus de Rubeis Formis R

appointed Ligorio architect to St Peter's in 1564 when Michelangelo died, but he abandoned the post in 1568 during the reign of Pius V Ghislieri (1504–72), elected in 1566, who was a stern reformer unsympathetic to antiquarian pursuits. Ligorio accordingly reaffirmed his allegiance to Ferrara with his appointment as antiquarian to Alfonso II d'Este (1533–97) Duke of Ferrara. Ligorio's example is indicative of the personal importance to architects of their particular patrons, and also a recognition of the special vagaries of papal patronage, which always ended abruptly. Instead, the Este patronage Ligorio had cultivated flourished and enabled him to undertake numerous projects including many temporary architectural settings in Ferrara. If a pope had been strategic and created powerful cardinal nephews, then his death did not always mean the end of the family's patronage. In the case of Paul III, quite the opposite occurred because the minor works they had previously undertaken in their native Lazio paled into insignificance with the magnificent patronage undertaken in Parma and Piacenza by Paul III's nephews after his death. The only important exception to established patterns of papal patronage occurred when members of the most significant single family of the entire Renaissance were elected to the See of Peter, as the patronage in their native city already rivalled that of papal Rome.

Florence and the Medici

The enormous prestige obtained from having two members of the family elected pope in close succession was consolidated during Clement VII's papacy in 1530, when the Medici returned from their three year exile to definitively regain rule over Florence. Both the despotic Alessandro and the great Cosimo I, who ruled from 1537–74, were made Dukes by Charles V, and Cosimo I became Grand Duke of Tuscany in 1569. His extensive patronage was aimed at enriching and refurbishing Medici residences such as the villa at Castello by Tribolo (1538–50), and with remodelling governmental buildings including the Palazzo Vecchio in which Cosimo I resided throughout the 1540s. He also commissioned new public buildings such as the Uffizi, executed by Vasari, who was appointed court artist in 1554, and who created a triumphal, celebratory architecture which helped to make Cosimo I's court one of the finest in Europe.

Vasari had an unusually good education, first in his native Arezzo where he studied Latin and learned to paint, and then in Florence where he continued his artistic training, and was edu-

50. Giorgio Vasari's own residence at Arezzo (1542–50) represents the social ambitions of the architect, painter and courtier. Vasari decorated the Sala del Cammino with various mythologies, including the Art of Painting allegory, demonstrating his erudition and wit. The status of artists and architects rose dramatically in the sixteenth century and Vasari became a highly valued member of the Medici court.

cated alongside Ippolito and Alessandro de' Medici. During the latter's rule, 1531–37, Vasari turned to the study of architecture and was first involved in creating ephemeral works. He helped to organize the temporary decorations for Charles V's Florentine entry of 1536, just as he had collaborated on his entry into Bologna of 1530. During his stay in Venice (1541–42) Vasari designed a temporary theatrical setting, including the painted *scenae frons*, in a palace interior for the first performance of Aretino's play *La Talanta*. Vasari then undertook the interior decoration of his own house at Arezzo (1542–50), based on his first-hand knowledge of the houses of Andrea Mantegna and Giulio in Mantua. He painted three erudite cycles, including one dedicated to Fame with figures representing Poetry, Painting, Architecture and Sculpture; another was dedicated to Apollo and the Muses. The principal room was dedicated to the Triumph of Virtue, but also contained scenes based on episodes from Pliny about the ancient painters Protogene, Apelles, Zeuxis and Timante, a particularly appropriate choice by Vasari who, urged on by the physician Paolo Giovio (1483–1552), composed in the same years the first proper history of art. Vasari's *Lives of the Artists*, which Giovio helped edit, first appeared in 1550 – the same year as the translation of the treatise of Alberti (1404–72) into Italian by Cosimo Bartoli (1503–72) – and in a much larger second edition in 1568 that contained seven additional chapters on architecture.

From 1555 onwards Vasari remodelled the interior of the Palazzo Vecchio as the principal seat of Ducal government. His first significant improvement was the construction from 1560 of a new staircase in the centre of the building which linked the ground floor entrance and courtyard to the Salone dei Cinquecento on the second floor. Vasari's staircase had a regular gradient of wide steps, and its walls and barrel-vaulted ceilings were whitewashed to reflect the light which entered from the strategically located diamond-shaped windows, designed to harmonize with the gradient of the flight. The staircase comprehensively divided the public and private spheres of the palace, and functioned well ceremonially because of the grandiose ascent via double ramps, surrounding the inner lightwell, that converged again before the entrance to the hall, conveniently located on the central cross-axis. Vasari also remodelled the Salone dei Cinquecento for ceremonial use by the Ducal court, fitting out with the classical orders the dais built earlier by Baccio Bandinelli (1493–1560). Vasari's technical abilities were demonstrated when he raised the ceiling height by several metres to enable the insertion of numerous windows, greatly increasing the interior illumination for the elaborate decorative cycle of paintings on the walls and the monumental ceiling. This provided the Florentines with an equivalent to Sangallo's Sala Regia in the Vatican and the Sala del Maggiore Consiglio in the Ducal Palace of Venice.

Vasari designed the Uffizi in 1559, to unite and house thirteen different government offices in this centralized location between the Palazzo Vecchio and the river Arno. Houses were demolished to lay out a street between the wings of the new building, flanked by the long ground-floor porticoes that provided access to the individual authorities. Vasari allocated each magistrate a separate suite of rooms in what constituted an office block. They occupied ground, mezzanine, and first floor, with individual offices having a width of three bays, clearly represented at

51. (Overleaf) The Uffizi complex in Florence (1559) is one of the most impressive urban projects of the sixteenth century. Vasari created a central street and lined it with continuous buildings to provide a coherence and continuity, while also distinguishing each of the various magistratures housed within the complex by their separate entrances under the porticoes, complete with seats for those waiting outside.

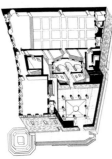

portico level by the piers interspersed with Doric columns that frame the entrance to each office in the portico. Yet it was the comprehensive integration of all these separate offices within a coherent overarching architectural framework disposed around the regularly articulated space of the square that created such a strong impression of a rationally ordered governmental space. The porticoes were carefully designed by Vasari to achieve powerful perspectival effects when standing within them, reinforcing the sense of logical spatial order, just as the whole square takes on the appearance of a carefully designed stage set.

After Vasari's death in 1574, work continued on the Uffizi under the direction of the Medici's new chief architect, Bernardo Buontalenti (1523–1608), who designed the elegantly licentious Porta delle Suppliche in 1577. The plain door jambs, flanked by recessed partial doric pilasters, are surmounted by a pediment that, contrary to all expectations, flares out from the centre like a pair of wings and is deliberately set against a contrasting, partial arched window. Buontalenti also transformed the third floor of the Uffizi into a museum, designing one of the first purpose-built rooms for the display of art, contemporary with the Gallery of Antiquities at Sabbioneta (pp. 00). The octagonal rotunda of the

54

52. Vasari's renovations to the Salone dei Cinquecento (left) in the Palazzo Vecchio in Florence (1560s) included raising the height of the roof and inserting extra windows for more light. The dais inserted at the eastern end of the room emphaszed the function of the hall as a place of government business.

53. Vasari also inserted a converging double ramp in the Palazzo Vecchio in Florence (1560s) which led to the Salone dei Cinquecento and which established a monumental approach to the hall, as can be seen in this diagram.

Tribuna (1581–86) is lit from above by windows in the drum, and this beautiful room became the archetypal museum and gallery space. In 1586, for the wedding of Virginia de' Medici and Cesare d'Este (1562–1628), Buontalenti further transformed the third storey of the Uffizi by creating a theatre to hold 3000 people, and designed the stage sets for the first of many *intermezzi* held there, including the spectacular month-long celebrations in 1589 to celebrate the wedding of Grand Duke Ferdinand I de' Medici (1549–1609) and Princess Christina of Lorraine.

For the protection of Cosimo I, Vasari linked, by way of an ele-

54. The Porta delle Suppliche in Florence (1577) by Bernardo Buontalenti is one of the most elegant doorways ever created.

55. Bartolomeo Ammannati designed the Ponte Santa Trìnita in Florence (1558–70) to be structurally sound yet appear elegant and almost insubstantial at the high point of each arch.

vated corridor, the Palazzo Vecchio and the Uffizi with the grounds of the Pitti Palace, following its purchase in 1549 by Eleonora of Toledo (1522–62) when it became the principal Ducal residence. Built in 1565, this corridor is a good example of utilitarian architecture, conceived without recourse to the orders, and is evidence of how, with the necessary technical skills, new construction could be summarily imposed onto existing buildings. Beyond the Uffizi the corridor traverses the street, where it is set upon a tall arcade that effectively blocks the view from and of existing palaces, and continues along the line of the river bank towards the Ponte Vecchio, which it also traverses above existing shops. The random shape and size of the older shops contrasts dramatically with the regularity of the corridor that surmounts them. This odd architectural amalgam also presents a dramatic contrast to the strong clean lines of the new bridge that spanned the Arno a short distance away, near the church of the Santa Trìnita. Following Michelangelo's initial involvement in 1560, the bridge was executed from 1567 to 1578 by his esteemed friend, the sculptor and architect Ammannati, who had practised widely in Venice and the Veneto 1527–32, Naples 1536–38, and Rome 1550–55, before returning to his native Tuscany and settling in Florence in 1555. Ammannati employed his formidable technical skills to design and execute this beautiful bridge with its shallow elliptical arches which spring tautly from solid pier to solid pier, while the elegant line of the parapet wall appears to be stretched from river bank to river bank.

In the 1560s Ammannati added two wings to the Pitti Palace to form a courtyard on the garden front and, inspired by the façade of the palace, created an elevational treatment that is a

55

56

56. Ammannati also built the courtyard and garden front of the Palazzo Pitti in Florence (1560s) revetting the exterior with a complete set of rusticated orders.

57. The courtyard of the Granducal residence of Palazzo Pitti was also used for entertainments including a *naumachia* organized by Buontalenti and recorded in this drawing by Orazio Scarabelli (1589).

symphony of rustication – even the Doric, Ionic and Corinthian semi-columns of the three storeys have rusticated banding. Rustication was appropriate for a façade that gave onto the gardens, entered via twin tunnel-like ramps from the courtyard, that were begun in 1549 by Tribolo, following his successful garden designs for the Medici villa at Castello in the 1540s. The Pitti Palace courtyard also functioned as a theatre – viewed from both the palace and the garden – for the many spectacles such as that organized by Buontalenti during the wedding festivities of 1589, when he recreated an ancient *naumachia* by flooding the courtyard and setting boats afloat there. This marvellous spectacle depended on both Buontalenti's design and engineering skills, as did the water supplies needed for the fountains at the Boboli gardens, and for Medici residences such as the villa and gardens of Pratolino, designed in 1569 for Francesco I Medici (1541–87) who ruled from 1574. Buontalenti also designed and

57

120

completed in the 1580s the upper half of Vasari's Grotto Grande adjacent to the Pitti Palace, that was actually a cistern which fed water to Florence, and in which Michelangelo's unfinished slaves from the tomb of Julius II were set within the rough stone grottowork of this artificial cave. License of this sort was usually taken up by architects in the context of temporary architecture where they felt able to engage in a type of creative design not permitted for permanent buildings. But in Florence in the 1560s and 1570s, when Vasari and Ammannati were bringing to completion the Library at San Lorenzo, and patrons favoured novelty above all, this distinction became negligible. After all, the foundation by Cosimo I in 1563 of the Florentine Academy of Design with Michelangelo as its 'Guide, Father and Master', well indicated the attitude towards Michelangelo's work in Florence. It was also the city in which, in the ecclesiastical field, Buontalenti was able to realise as late as 1574 his essay in licentiousness, the fantastic staircase for Santa Trìnita that has all the qualities of ephemera made permanent.

The highly sophisticated atmosphere of the Medici court was well represented by one of its most famous artists, Cellini, whose heterosexual relations were often sadistic; his homosexual exploits led to imprisonment, yet his several murders remained unprosecuted – by comparison, his short tract on architecture is a conventional restatement of earlier writings by others. Yet like the ephemeral decorations that were so popular, Cosimo I's libertine court rapidly evaporated – at least in public – notwithstanding Buontalenti's work. The Reformation had a distinct impact on his policies in the ecclesiastical field because he was in pursuit of the Granducal title which was the pope's to award. Cosimo I took up in public the reforming spirit advocated by Pius V and personally sponsored Vasari's renovations of Santa Maria Novella and Santa Croce, duly receiving the title of Grand Duke in 1569. Vasari removed traditional structures including rood-screens, *ponte* and *tramezzi*, which divided the clergy and laity in these mendicant churches, and returned to the ideals of the simple, open interior spaces of the early Christian church where the altar was fully visible to the faithful from the nave. The mood of the Catholic Restoration was taken seriously by Ammannati who became extremely religious and even composed a letter to the Florentine Academy of Design in 1582 in which he attacked the nudity of many public sculptures. Attitudes had indeed changed and even Ammannati's design of 1579 for the Jesuit church and college of San Giovannino was rejected as being too sumptuous, despite being modelled on the Gesù in Rome.

Architects designing palaces in the late sixteenth century also returned to the austerity and sobriety of the earlier part of the century, exemplified by the Bartolini-Salimbeni palace built 1520–23 by Baccio d'Agnolo (1462–1543) of the Baglioni family of architects that included Giuliano (1491–1555) and Domenico (1510–54). Apart from the exceptional palace for Giovanni Uguccioni of 1549 situated on the Piazza della Signoria in front of the Palazzo Vecchio, which had a façade with a full complement of the orders, later palaces such as the Palazzo Zanchini of 1583 by Santi di Tito (1536–1603) and the Palazzo Giacomini of 1580 by Giovan Antonio Dosio (1533–1609) remained true to the tradition of rusticated quoins at the flanks of the façade rising to a strongly projecting cornice, and a façade consisting of three pedimented windows on each storey – the principal entrance seems merely to be a window that descends to ground level. Dosio strategically located the interior courtyard away from the street, thus maintaining a solid exterior while providing light and air for the interior, but his design remained limited by the narrow, vertical, corner site, and also by the traditionally consistent height of Florentine palaces throughout the city where Brunelleschi's dome dominated all. The city's flat plain offered fewer possibilities for innovative palace design than the inherent opportunities available in cities with dramatic sloping hills.

Genoa and Milan

After Andrea Doria I (1466–1560) liberated Genoa from French domination in 1527, he commissioned a new residence from Perino del Vaga (1501–47) who decorated it in the High Renaissance style of his late master Raphael. The long, low two-storey building may be considered an early example of a suburban villa, located as it was on the outskirts of town, on a shallow site between the sea and the steeply rising mountains behind. The villa commanded spectacular views of the port, perfectly appropriate for the Admiral who presided over Genoa's rebirth in the 1530s as an independent centre of commerce and finance. Doria was the first of the re-established succession of Doges who ruled Genoa for two-year periods, selected from the families of the old nobility such as the Grimaldi, Spinola, and Giustiniani, who were also the most significant patrons of the period.

Galeazzo Alessi (1512–72) worked in Rome during Paul III's

58, 59. Galeazzo Alessi designed this impressive villa, set on one of the many hills surrounding Genoa, for the Giustiniani family (1548). The *piano nobile* loggia to the rear of the villa affords fine sea views.

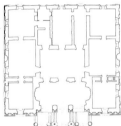

60. The Strada Nuova in Genoa (1550s) is one of the most impressive Italian streets of the sixteenth century, with grand palaces lining it to create an attractive aristocratic residential area that contrasted strongly with the narrow meandering medieval streets in the rest of the city.

papacy, returning to his native Perugia in 1542 to execute the fortifications of the Rocca Paolina designed by Sangallo. There he met members of the Genoese Sauli family, including Bartolomeo, who was Apostolic Treasurer of Perugia and Umbria, and Cardinal Girolamo, who persuaded Alessi to move to Genoa in 1548 to build a splendid new church to be paid for by the family. Santa Maria di Carignano was designed on a large Greek-cross plan, with a tall dome and corner towers that exploit its prominent location on the top of a hill (pp. 96–99). Alessi's next project also came via the Sauli family, related by marriage to Luca Giustiniani, who commissioned a villa, also situated on the top of a hill, where it dominated its surroundings and provided splendid views for its owners. The principal façade of the square block has three slightly receding central bays that house an enclosed ground floor Doric portico, which leads to an internal vestibule and staircase that ascends to a second enclosed loggia on the piano nobile with views of the bay of Genoa, and a large salone which extends to the principal façade. The axially

95

58, 59

symmetrical plan and compact massing of the villa are indebted to Palladio's achievements in the Veneto, but the internal ascent to the piano nobile and the elaborate interior stuccowork of herms and coffering established a new model for subsequent Genoese palace design. Alessi's Villa Grimaldi of 1552 and the Villa Pallavicino of 1555 both have complex internal room and stair arrangements and architectural elements that extend beyond the discrete block of the villa, respectively in the form of an atrium courtyard and a nymphaeum.

These freestanding monumental buildings on hilltop sites were well removed from the noise and dirt of Genoa's crowded centre, but traditional family palaces were in the centre of town. The high cost of land in large cities meant that buildings normally abutted one another, including palaces and churches, the façades of which continuously lined the narrow streets, interrupted only by street intersections. Given this tradition, yet inspired by the ideas of Alessi, in 1549 several families from the old nobility collectively petitioned the Comune for permission to undertake an urban residential project to provide a neighbourhood in which to erect new palaces for themselves. Known as the Strada Nuova, the street lined with regular building lots was laid 60 out above the existing city in 1550 by Bernardino Cantone (1505–c. 1580), the Comune's official architect. Building on the plots was delayed by the Corsican war of liberation 1551–58, but immediately afterwards several grandiose palaces were begun. Cantone designed palaces for Agostino Pallavicino and Angelo Spinola, and in collaboration with Giovanni Battista Castello (1509–69) for Tobia Pallavicino, Giambattista Spinola, and Nicolosia Lomellino, all begun between 1558 and 1563. These palaces uniformly lined the street so that the focus was on the interiors, which have unusual spatial sequences comprising vestibules which give directly onto open courtyards with unenclosed staircases leading to the piano nobile. These arrangements prefigured the grandest palace, commissioned by Nicolò Grimaldi in 1565 from the brothers Domenico and Giovanni Ponzello, and executed by the master mason Giovanni Lurago (d. 1571) in the local pink *finale* stone (pp. 113–4).

Alessi left for Milan in 1557 to execute a commission for a Genoese client, Tommaso Marino. Milan had been under Spanish domination since 1521 and Marino, who transferred there in 1523, was typical of the entrepreneurial business class the regime attracted: he ran a flourishing tax collection business which enabled him, by 1557, to expropriate the large plot of land

61. Alessi's first commission in Milan was the Palazzo Marini (1557) where he was able to fully express his skill in architectural ornament, lavished on the *piano nobile* of the courtyard. The ground floor portico is soberly articulated with Doric columns.

on which to build his palace. Immediately inside the entrance to the massive block is a large open two-storey courtyard, succeeded by a tall ground-floor salone that separates the courtyard from the garden wings which contained the apartments of the patron's two sons. The courtyard is composed of serliana arcades, surmounted by arches on the piano nobile separated by wide, richly decorated piers with herms replacing the orders. Unlike Alessi's Genoese buildings, where such decoration was generally confined to interior stucco work, here it was perfectly

61

62. Leone Leoni's own residence in Milan is known as the House of the Omenoni (1565) because of the six terms on the façade.

63. Domenico Giunti's Villa La Gonzaga (1547) on the outskirts of Milan exemplifies how archaeology influenced sixteenth-century architecture as the façade is clearly based on the ancient Roman Septizonium. The arcaded ground floor is surmounted by a tall loggia on the *piano nobile* while the second floor loggia terminates with a hipped roof rather than an entablature and cornice.

in tune with the wealth of exterior ornamental decoration traditionally employed in Lombard architecture. Alessi's Palazzo Marino had a direct influence on the Palazzo dei Giureconsulti of 1561 designed by Vincenzo Seregni (1504/9–94), who also employed serliana arcading on the ground floor, an effective device because of the feeling of lightness and airiness it created, especially under the vaulted arcades. The most notable example of exterior decoration was by the bronze sculptor Leone Leoni (1509–90) for the façade of his house. Leoni, who had been made a knight by Charles V in 1549 after a very chequered career, designed his House of the Omenoni in 1565 with a pair of caryatids flanking the entrance and six colossal herms of barbarian prisoners bound to and suspended from their pilasters as they have been amputated below the knees. Leoni based his caryatids on those of a victory portico illustrated in the 1556 edition of Vitruvius by Daniele Barbaro, a good example of an architect responding to the antique via a contemporary source.

Equally based on antique, but very different, models and yielding different results, was the suburban villa La Gonzaga remodelled by Domenico Giunti (1505–60), following its purchase by Ferrante Gonzaga (1507–57) when he became Governor of Milan in 1546. Giunti added wings to the garden front to create a courtyard with ground floor arcading succeeded by two fishponds described as *nymphaea* and decorated with stuccoes, marbles and frescoes. For the principal façade, Giunti turned to the ancient Roman model of the Septizonium to create a soberly articulated three-storey loggia. Monumental austerity

62

63

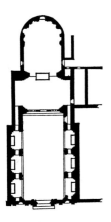

64, 65. Because Alessi's unusual plan for Santi Paolo e Barnaba in Milan (1558) comprises a nave but no aisles, attention is focused on the chancel and high altar.

66. Both Seregni and Alessi worked at San Vittore al Corpo in Milan (1553–64) where an unusual crossing flanked by apsidal transepts is succeeded by a chancel and monks' choir. Tibaldi modified and completed the church (1568).

67. The austere double-storey courtyard of Tibaldi's Collegio Borromeo at Pavia (1564–89), with its repeated Serlian arcading, was inspired by Alessi's Palazzo Marini.

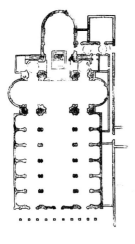

also characterized Giunti's church of Sant'Angelo of 1552, and his unrealized proposal for the façade of Santa Maria presso San Celso of the early 1550s – inspired by the austere drum and dome of Santa Maria della Passione built in 1530 by Cristoforo Lombardo (1480/90–1555). By comparison, Alessi's design for the façade of Santa Maria presso San Celso of 1565–68 displayed 64, 65 a striking combination of architectural and sculptural elements.

Alessi's most significant achievement was in the field of church planning where he developed innovative and influential schemes. The Barnabite order was founded in Milan in 1530 and was sponsored by Domenico Sauli, whose son Alessandro was a member of the order. In 1547 the order undertook the renovation of their church dedicated to Saints Paolo and Barnaba, but after being granted official recognition by Paul IV in 1556, the order commissioned a new church on the same site. In 1558 Alessi provided a design that was only approved in 1561, but it is an innovative church that established clear and functional spatial divisions in a remarkable arrangement. Three chapels, separated by balustrades and raised upon steps, open directly onto the aisless nave at each side; these chapels are connected by passageways which link them to the domed chancel space, which is otherwise separated from the lay space of the nave by steps, balustrades, and the projecting respondent piers and arch; the high altar is situated at the rear of the chancel and at the beginning of the choir for the conventuals. This innovative plan influenced the design of San Vittore al Corpo for the Olevetan Order, where Seregni had 66

70

worked from 1553, and where Alessi was involved around 1564. The wide-bodied church consists of a nave, aisles and side chapels decorated with rich Alessian coffering, succeeded by a crossing flooded with light from the dome. The apsidal transepts project beyond the body of the church and again the high altar is located on the threshold between the chancel and the choir of the conventuals. The design of the upper portions of San Vittore was modified and completed by Pellegrino Tibaldi (1527–96) in 1568, thus establishing a direct link between these innovative churches of the late 1550s and early 1560s and the work of Tibaldi for Charles Borromeo (1538–84) in the 1560s and 1570s.

Borromeo was called to Rome, made a Cardinal, and designated Archbishop of Milan in 1560 by his uncle Pius IV. He was active as Cardinal-nephew in bringing the 1562–63 sessions of the Council of Trent to a conclusion, enabling Pius IV to promulgate the decrees in 1564. Either in Ancona or Rome he met Tibaldi, who had previously worked in Emilia and the Romagna, and whom Borromeo set to work in his extensive Milanese diocese in 1561, where Tibaldi's first task was the construction of the Collegio Borromeo in Pavia, for the education of secular priests, built 1564–89. In 1564 Borromeo took up his post in Milan and greatly encouraged the New Orders, although he had the unsatisfactory Umiliati disbanded in 1569. He promoted their programme of church-building and renovation that coincided with his own aims for reform. He personally instigated pastoral visits to the churches of his diocese in order to remedy unsatisfactory arrangements in them, and these visits proved a powerful and effective instrument during his reign. Borromeo was often accompanied on these visits by Tibaldi, and their strong working relationship resulted in Tibaldi becoming in effect Borromeo's personal architect. Their respective architectural and theoretical contributions were together united in creating an innovative ecclesiastical architecture that symbolized the reformed church. At Borromeo's insistence, in 1567 Tibaldi, who was already a founding member of the Milan College of Engineers and Architects, was also appointed architect of the cathedral, replacing Seregni, whose design for the renewal of the square in front of the cathedral of 1548 was never realized. From 1568 onwards Tibaldi not only renovated the Archbishop's Palace, including the Canonica in 1572, but installed in the cathedral classicizing altars in the nave, a canopy over the baptismal font, and the layered steps leading to the chancel and high altar. He also designed the extraordinary circular crypt with a

67

68

ring of columns and surrounding ambulatory based on the Early Christian mausoleum later dedicated as a church to Santa Costanza, in Rome. Conservative opposition to Tibaldi's project was led by Martino Bassi (1541–91) who collected opinions from Palladio, Vasari and Vignola and published them in 1572, but to no avail, as Tibaldi's work in Milan Cathedral perfectly represented Borromeo's views regarding the proper restoration of ecclesiastical architecture. By the 1570s, Borromeo had great practical experience from administering his diocese, and having formulated his ideas regarding the constitution of good church design, in 1577 published his *Instructions for ecclesiastical buildings and furnishings*. This was not an architectural treatise, but it clearly indicated exactly how he believed churches should be built and furnished, including simple advice such as siting the church on a hill or raising it on a plinth to increase its magnificence. Borromeo's writing became highly influential because of its clarity and its simple structure in thirty-three chapters covering everything from the site and design of a church, to its main altar, choir, lamps and seating. His handbook excluded architecture, which Borromeo said he would leave to others, but it was ideally complemented by the three-part treatise composed in the 1590s by Tibaldi. This included commentaries on the treatises of Vitruvius and Alberti, and forty-three sections setting out the most important public buildings required in a city: Basilica, Curia, Senator's Palace, Palace of Justice, Prison, Treasury, Mint, Armoury, Library, Cathedral, Bishop's Palace, Canon's House, Seminary, Churches, Lawyers and Notaries College, Medical College, Theatre, School, Hospital, Palestra, Baths and Pools, Stables, Granaries, Market, Meatmarket, Salt Warehouse.

Chapter 2:   Urbanism, building types and treatises

Urbanism and fortifications

Urbanism and architecture are deeply interrelated, as interventions in the urban fabric of a city provide the impetus for architectural renewal, while large-scale architectural projects often change the surrounding urban fabric. The construction of fortifications, whether surrounding a city as part of the walls or protecting sea-ports, exemplifies the integral relation between architecture and urbanism.

Important examples occur in the Spanish-ruled South, where the first Viceroy, Don Ferrante Gonzaga, transformed the coastline of Sicily through the construction from the 1540s onwards of 137 fortified watch-towers; the entire career of Ambrogio Attendolo (1515–85) was spent inspecting and maintaining the fortifications of the kingdom of Naples. The Viceroys of Naples, Don Pedro de Toledo who ruled 1532–53, and Don Afan de Ribera 1559–68, built 360 fortified watch-towers along the Neapolitan coast; in 1536 Don Pedro also had the via Toledo constructed through the heart of Naples to provide a thoroughfare for his troops as they moved between the port, their housing in the newly constructed Spanish Quarter, and the fortress of Sant'Elmo, built 1537–46 by Pedro Luis Scrivà (active 1530–96) to the latest star shaped designs. In the case of Naples, like that of Turin, major urban and architectural renewal was the result of military planning and construction.

In the sixteenth century architects mainly found employment because of their skills in engineering and fortification design, as the livelihood of a city and its inhabitants depended on these. The invention, at the end of the fifteenth century, of the iron cannonball that could destroy traditional fortifications made redundant the round towers recommended by Vitruvius and hitherto used extensively. These were replaced by the more technologically advanced triangular bastion, a projecting gun platform from whose impregnably protected re-entrant angles artillery-fire parallel to the curtain wall could destroy the enemy before it could breach the fort. This innovation was first created by Sangallo's father, and his cousin, for the Roman bastions at Civita Castellana of 1495 and Nettuno of 1501.It was further developed by Sangallo at the Fortezza da Basso of Florence in 1534, and at the Bastione Ardeatino of 1537 commissioned by Paul III in the aftermath of the Sack of Rome, that had

69. The double-storey white Istrian stone screen that Palladio designed to transform the original building into his Basilica (1549) in the main square of Vicenza is revealed in this aerial photograph. Palladio's work influenced the design on the Palazzo della Loggia of Brescia executed by Ludovico Beretta (1550–74) and the impressive Palazzo della Gran Guardia in Verona designed by Domenico Curtoni (1609).

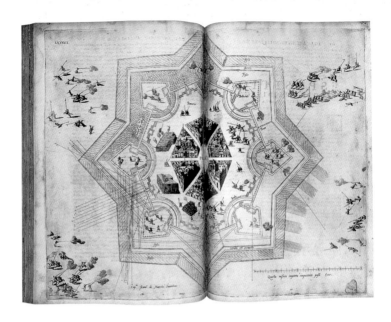

70. Francesco de' Marchi's treatise on fortifications (1599) included a series of engraved plates depicting various forms of angled bastions and explaining how they functioned.

shown up the weaknesses of the city's fortifications. Peruzzi also adopted the triangular bastion when repairing and rebuilding the fortifications of his native Siena in his role of architect to the Republic. Subsequent works in Siena, such as the Spanish Citadel of 1550 by Giovanni Battista Peloro (1483–1558), also employed this new technology, although the city was conquered by Florence in 1557.

After the Sack, Michelangelo left the service of Clement VII, whose numerous projects in the papal states were executed by Pierfrancesco da Viterbo (1470–1537). The Republican Michelangelo returned to Florence where he became governor-general of fortifications in 1529 and designed extraordinary zoomorphic plans which were never realised. More practically, for Cosimo I, Cellini and Giovanni Battista Belluzzi (1506–54) renewed the city walls (1552–54) and defences throughout Tuscany, while Buontalenti, who built the Belvedere fortress (1590–95), also designed the fortifications and harbour at the great port of Livorno in 1576 as part of the project of urban renewal undertaken there by Ferdinando I de' Medici.

Military writing was extensive, from Nicolò Macchiavelli's *The Art of War* 1522 to the 1540 treatise by Vannuccio Biringucci (1480–1537) *On Fireworks* that included important observations about artillery, based on his knowledge of scientific developments in metallurgy. Serlio's unpublished eighth book was

71. The fortifications that encircle the city of Lucca were designed to circumscribe the existing medieval city with modern star-bastions.

devoted to classical military camps, and most architectural treatises, such as the *First Four Books of Architecture* of 1554 by Pietro Cataneo (1500–69), discussed fortifications at length. A veritable explosion of specialized literature was written by architects and military engineers and soldiers including Giovanbattista Zanchi (1554), Girolamo Cataneo (1564), Galeazzo Alessi (1564–70), Carlo Theti (1569), Antonio Lupicini (1582), Giovan Battista Belluzzi (1598), Francesco de' Marchi (1599), Gabrio Busca (1601), Giovanni Botero (1601), Giovan Francesco Fiammelli (1604 and 1606), Francesco Tensini (1623), and Matteo Oddi (1627). One of the most sought after military engineers, Galasso Alghisi (*c.* 1523–73), published a theoretical treatise in three volumes in 1570, after settling in Ferrara in 1558 and working for Ercole II (1508–59) and Alfonso II d'Este. Alghisi's treatise marked the culmination of a distinguished career which included advising Paul III about refortifying the Roman Borgo, and Margaret of Austria (1522–86) about her palace at Piacenza. (Margaret had several surnames including Farnese, because she was the natural daughter of Emperor Charles V, married Duke Alessandro de' Medici (assassinated 1537), inherited the Palazzo and Villa Madama in Rome, and in 1538 married Ottavio Farnese (1524–86) and later embarked on building the Palazzo Farnese in Piacenza.) Apart from locals such as Smeraldo Smeraldi (1553–1634), many architects and

70

72. Antonio da Ponte's practical
design for the Rialto Bridge
(1588) consisted of a single broad
arch that enabled even large and
broad boats to pass underneath.
The numerous shops that line
the interior street provide rental
income and the outer staircases
allow pedestrians to cross the
bridge without entering
the crowded central area.

engineers were also called to Parma and Piacenza to provide defensive and civic structures for Dukes Ottavio and Alessandro Farnese (1520–89), including the remarkable military architect Francesco Paciotto (1521–91) of Urbino. Paciotto, who designed the Citadella of Parma in 1556, was ennobled in 1578 after a series of appointments from Julius III, Pius V, Emperor Philip II and Duke Emanuele Filiberto of Savoy (1533–80).

In 1561 Paciotti was involved in the design and construction of a new series of fortified walls which enclose the city of Lucca and which were begun in 1544 by Jacopo Seghizzi (c. 1484–c. 1565) and Baldassare Lanci (1510–71); they demonstrate the difference between the theory and practice of fortification. The location and angle of the fortified walls between the bastions were determined by the presence of existing buildings, and were not generated solely through recourse to ideal geometrical figures, as was the military town of Palmanova, laid out from 1593 principally by Giulio Savorgnan (1516–90) and Bonaiuto Lorini (c. 1540–1611). Palmanova has a hexagonal central piazza from which streets radiate out to alternate gates and bastions located on the regular polygonal eighteen-sided perimeter wall that appears to have been copied directly from a treatise such as that of 1595 by Francesco de' Marchi, and imposed indiscriminately on a location without concern for geography. Palmanova was unusual: most cities had fortified walls that were built over a long period of time.

Because bridges were an integral part of urban planning – often linking two halves of a city and therefore of strategic military significance – when architects came to design them they

73. The seven pilgrimage basilicas of Rome were represented in several engravings including this example published by Antoine Lafréry for the Jubilee (1575). Pilgrimage and ceremonial processions were a feature of everyday life in the sixteenth and seventeenth centuries in Rome and other Italian cities.

had to take into account existing conditions of terrain and extant building. Structural requirements and technological capability were usually the architect's most important considerations, exemplified by the Ponte Santa Trìnita in Florence and the new Rialto Bridge in Venice, which represented a victory of practicality and technology over architecture based on the classical orders. In the 1550s and 1560s Palladio had presented two schemes for rebuilding the Rialto bridge with a structure comprising three round-headed Roman arches supporting a classicizing loggia structure. Neither project was accepted because they took no account of the specialized topography of the Grand Canal and might have been built anywhere – except on the Grand Canal, where the low arches would have prevented all but the smallest boats from passing underneath. By comparison, Vincenzo Scamozzi (1548–1616), who first proposed a classical three-arch bridge similar to Palladio's, subsequently presented a design for a single non-classical arch that spanned the Grand Canal, and that was very close to the bridge as built by the aptly named Antonio da Ponte (1512–1597). With its competent structural engineering, including innovative underwater foundations, and the practical rows of internal shops set on a gentle gradient of stairs, Da Ponte designed a bridge that has remained without structural problems or subsidence for four hundred years in the uniquely difficult conditions of Venice.

Apart from enabling the passage of people and goods across cities divided by water, bridges had an inherently theatrical

55

142

72

81

potential as the people crossing them could see and be seen by those on the water and the river bank. So too, interventions such as the Strada Nuova in Genoa established an urban architecture in which sequential, processional, and stage-like qualities were emphasized. These qualities were also developed in architecture built for religious pilgrimage, such as the processional sites of the Sacro Monte of Varallo and that at Varese. When Alessi was commissioned in 1565 by Giacomo d'Adda to restructure Varallo, he produced a scheme comprising 34 chapels on the hillside, linked by pathways, so as to relate in a sequential narrative form to the pilgrim undertaking the ascent, the Biblical story from the Fall of Adam and Eve to the Last Judgement (represented by plaster figures arranged in the carefully designed

74. This bird's-eye city plan of Palermo (1686) depicts the fortifications surrounding the city, the three principal land entrances through gates in the walls, and the two major streets (1560s and 1590s) that divide the city into four quarters meeting at the Quattro Canti, with palaces executed by Giulio Lasso (1609–20).

75. Andrea Vicentino recorded the splendid ceremonial entry into Venice (1574) of King Henry III of France, when Palladio designed the temporary triumphal arch and loggia on the Lido.

architectural settings of the chapel interiors). Alessi's elaborate scheme was recorded in a series of designs known as the *Libro dei Misteri* 1565–69, but it was only partially executed because it conflicted with the increasingly austere spirit of reform. D'Adda subsequently had Bassi simplify the scheme and, on the initiative of Carlo Bascapè, Bishop of Novara from 1593, many further chapels were executed. The display of reformation values reached rhetorical heights when patrons constructed Sacri Monti on the approach to their villas, such as that of the Villa Duodo at Monselice of 1605.

Christian pilgrimage on a much larger scale was taken up enthusiastically by the energetic Sixtus V Peretti (1520–90) on his election in 1585. He set about transforming Rome and the Curia to such an extent that in just five years he had restructured the papal administration and literally changed the face of the city, with the help of his trusted architect Domenico Fontana (1543–1607). Sixtus V recognized the primary importance of Rome for pilgrims, and his most effective idea was to commission the placement of 'Christianized' obelisks (surmounted with crosses) in front of the major pilgrimage basilicas in Rome. He had the basilicas connected by newly constructed or greatly improved streets, and the obelisks functioned as tall signposts for pilgrims approaching from a distance. Such decisive urban interventions, that relied on the ability to create new streets, could only be undertaken by powerful rulers who were able to impose their vision on a city; Sixtus V's project involved legislation that was imposed on private landowners but resulted in spectacular improvements to the urban layout of Rome, includ-

73

ing the magnificent Quattro Fontane crossroads. There the respective thoroughfares converged and were decorated with fountains in each corner, and from this central vantage point wonderful views through the city on four axes were created.

A similar strategy was employed to great effect in Palermo where the via Toledo, constructed in the 1560s to connect 74 the Royal Palace to the sea, intersected with the via Maqueda, built in the 1590s to form the Quattro Canti. New palaces erected on this crossroad from 1609 by Giulio Lasso had fountains at ground level with statues representing the four seasons. Urban interventions such as the Quattro Canti were politically symbolic, and the piano nobile façades have statues of the ruling Spanish kings. These wide thoroughfares through the heart of the city culminated in city gates that were often the starting point of ceremonial entries. These processions began on the periphery of the city and moved towards the public buildings at its heart, using temporary architecture to brilliant effect in these urban spaces. Throughout Italy ceremonial entries took similar forms, but in Venice they took on a special aspect being partially based on the water, as in the 1574 entry of King

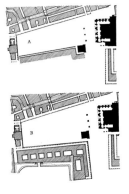

Henry III of France at the Lido of Venice for which Palladio   75
designed an arch and loggia. A second arch was constructed at
the water entrance to Piazza San Marco at the centre of the city,
but little else was required because the festivities made use of
the permanent stage-like setting already established there by
Palladio's predecessor.

Public buildings

Reconstructing public buildings situated on the main square of a
city often provided the opportunity for an architect to alter the
relationship between a building and the space surrounding it in
favour of increased architectural regularity and visual order. A   76, 77
good example is Sansovino's project for urban renewal undertaken in Piazza San Marco at the instigation of Doge Gritti.
Sansovino widened the piazza towards the church and Ducal
Palace by bringing further south the alignment of the Procuratie
Nuove and Library and separating their horizontal masses from
the previously enclosed bell-tower. Palladio considered
Sansovino's Library one of the finest buildings since antiquity,
and it clearly provided the inspiration for his proposed remodel-   69
ling of the medieval town hall structure in Vicenza, which was
chosen in 1549 in preference to designs presented by Sanmicheli,
Giulio Romano, Sansovino, and Serlio. Palladio seized the opportunity to recreate an ancient basilica, or public hall, and he created an impressive classicizing architectural screen of apparent
regularity, but which in reality had individual serliana openings
all of slightly, if imperceptibly, different lengths, caused by the
presence of the earlier building.

In general, existing buildings were refurbished or incorporated into new projects rather than demolished, and even
Palladio's expensive, carved stone screen cost much less than
rebuilding from scratch. So too, Vignola devised a regular façade
for the various buildings and streets on the east side of the Piazza   80
Maggiore of Bologna. His Portico dei Banchi of 1561 also provided an architecturally dignified and covered passageway that
offered protection from the elements at ground level, as did
Vasari's magnificent barrel-vaulted Uffizi porticoes, with which
he created a coherently articulated elongated piazza.
Michelangelo aimed to achieve similar effects when remodelling   78
the Campidoglio for Paul III from 1539 onwards, and he took up
the challenge to rival the ancients in the adjacent Forum
Romanum and designed a piazza and surrounding buildings
worthy of the title of Capitol – *caput totius mundi*. The existing

76, 77. The Piazza S. Marco,
Venice: the lower plan shows
how Sansovino set back the
corner of the Library (1537)
to liberate it from the bell-tower,
thus enlarging and altering the
plan of the Piazza shown in the
upper plan. Sansovino designed
three distinctly different buildings
for the Piazza: the Mint
(1536),the small, elegant
Loggia built of richly coloured
marbles (1537) and the Library
(1537), seen below left.

78, 79. Michelangelo's project for the Campidoglio in Rome, adjacent to the Forum Romanum, was engraved by Etienne Dupérac (1569). It consisted of two matching governmental palaces, one for the Conservators and one for the Senators. The only surviving antique bronze equestrian statue in Rome, that of Marcus Aurelius, was set in the middle of the oval pavement of the piazza. Like the Palazzo dei Conservatori (1563–84), the matching Palazzo Nuovo was built of local travertine and brick (1603–54).

Senator's Palace at the rear of the square was given a double staircase ascending to a new entrance on the first floor, and the two upper storeys were articulated with giant order pilasters. Michelangelo also employed giant order pilasters for the new Palazzo dei Conservatori to the west where they link the ground floor portico with the upper floor, establishing powerful vertical elements to balance the strong horizontal mass of the building. Michelangelo housed the Marcus Aurelius statue on a plinth at the centre of the oval piazza, which seems to float in the centre of the imperceptibly irregular trapezoidal space of the square, overwhelmed by the power of the architectural forms that enclose it.

Other types of public building found in a city included those dedicated to education, such as university buildings, religious colleges, and libraries. Universities followed the conventional monastic model of a centralized courtyard surrounded by double-storey loggias first established by Moroni for the University of Padua in the 1540s. In Bologna the Archiginnasio – university – was commissioned in 1561 by Pius IV to house the legal and artistic schools of the city. Antonio Terribilia (1500–1568) located the classrooms on the upper floor, above ground floor shops that provided rental income. So too, in Rome the Palazzo of the Sapienza was purpose-built for teaching, by numerous architects including Ligorio, Guidetto Guidetti (*c.* 1495–1564), Giacomo della Porta (1533–1602), and eventually Borromini, who designed the church of Sant'Ivo alla Sapienza. By contrast, in Ferrara Giovan Battista Aleotti (1546–1636) and Alessandro Balbi (1530–1604) transformed the existing Palazzo Paradiso acquired by Cardinal Luigi d'Este in 1586 into the seat of the University between 1598 and 1610, through the addition of a magnificent new façade and tower. There were, however, practical limits to the transformation and reuse of existing buildings, and often specific requirements rendered them unsatisfactory. The Jesuits eventually demolished and rebuilt from scratch their College in Rome to a design which specifically provided for one-hundred bedrooms, lecture halls, a library and various other rooms. They purchased adjacent land to accommodate their new building for which several architects presented projects. One particularly interesting proposal combined the expected regularity of a rectangular courtyard and surrounding rooms with an unusual hexagonal cloister that exploited the irregularity of the perimeter of the site while maintaining an internal consistency and variety of room shape. Libraries were an essential part of colleges and universities, with important manuscript collec-

203

80. Vignola's masterful composition for the Portico dei Banchi in Bologna (begun 1561) consists of a lower storey with giant pilasters that unites the ground floor arcades and the mezzanines above, and a first storey with triple windows in each compartment surmounted by smaller mezzanine windows, thus creating the appearance of just two main storeys.

81. Lelio Buzzi, Fabio Mangone and Giovanni Maria Ricchino were all involved in designing and building the Biblioteca Ambrosiana in Milan (begun 1603). The barrel-vaulted interior, lit by thermal windows at either end, is imbued with a sense of openness and uncluttered space, as the bookshelves line the walls but do not project into the volume of the reading room.

tions and, from the end of the fifteenth century, printed books. Compared with the Medici Library at San Lorenzo where books were housed on the reading desks, Fontana's Vatican Library of 1587–90 and the Biblioteca Ambrosiana in Milan, built from 1603 by Lelio Buzzi (1553–c. 1626) and others, represented a new type of library with shelving located against the walls, based on the Library at the Escorial, built in 1567 by Juan de Herrera (1530–97) for Philip II, who ruled over Milan 1556–98. Whereas the Vatican library had elaborate frescoed vaults above the shelves, at the Ambrosiana the shelves were of double height and reached to just below the barrel vault, thereby housing twice as many books.

82. Vincenzo Scamozzi's design for the hospital and church of San Lazzaro dei Mendicanti in Venice (1601) was adapted and transformed into a model that was then executed by Tommaso Contin (1605–36). The project takes up the traditional plan of matching twin cloisters, as seen in those adjacent at Santi Giovanni e Paolo in the lower half of the photograph. Scamozzi inserted the church of San Lazzaro between the two cloisters in the distance. Sangallo had devised a similar solution in his unbuilt project for San Giacomo in Augusta in Rome (c. 1538).

83. By comparison the plan of Sansovino's Hospital of the Incurabili in Venice (begun 1565, destroyed 1831) depicts the plan of the oval church he set in the middle of the cloister.

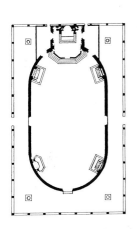

Hospitals were also based on traditional monastic plans, acknowledging their common provenance and continuing part in religious life, although civic hospitals administered by communes were developed, as were military hospitals such as that of San Giacomo, built in the military quarter of the same name in Palermo in the 1560s. Sangallo's unrealised plan of 1540 for the Incurables hospital and church of San Giacomo in Augusta in Rome envisaged twin cloisters separated by the church, situated on a central axis. This type of plan was eventually realised by Francesco da Volterra (c. 1530–94) in the early 1590s, and was also the basis of Scamozzi's design for the hospital and church of San Lazzaro dei Mendicanti in Venice of 1601, where the wings for men and women are situated around separate but identical courtyards located either side of the church. Sansovino's earlier Venetian hospital of the Incurabili, designed in 1565, was one of few innovative designs comprising an oval church in the centre of a rectangular courtyard. It was only in the late sixteenth century that hospitals began to perform exclusively the specialized function of caring for the sick, the senile, and the insane – although there had long been separate hospitals for lepers. Hospitals continued to act as hospices, and to care for foundlings and orphans, widows and the destitute – they even temporarily housed pilgrims.

The Reformation gave renewed impetus to specialized religious confraternities that offered poor relief on a local communi-

84. Giovan Battista Cavagna designed the Monte di Pietà in Naples (1599) with an austere central courtyard enriched by the ornate façade of the chapel located opposite the entrance from the street.

ty level, and to communal charitable institutions such as the Monti di Pietà that had been promoted by the Franciscans from the mid-fifteenth century onwards because they offered a means of alleviating the problems associated with money-lending and usury. Unlike the numerous banks established in the period, the Monti di Pietà were essentially Christian pawnshops that offered low-interest loans and, like nearly every public building of the period, included a chapel for worship. The example at Naples, designed in 1599 by Giovan Battista Cavagna (d. 1613) has a chapel façade distinguished architecturally from the rest of the institution by the richness of the Ionic pilasters, frieze and pediment, and the charitable activities took place in the principal hall located directly above the chapel. Another important example was the Monte di Pietà at Palermo, designed by Natale Masuccio (1561–c. 1630) in 1616. Public banks were also established at this time, including the bank at the Rialto in Venice in 1587, the Santo Spirito bank in Rome in 1591, and the bank of Sant'Ambrogio in Milan in 1593.

The incarcerated were also provided with specialized accommodation in purpose-built prisons such as that in Milan designed in 1578 by Pier Antonio Barca (d. 1636). Previously, prisoners were normally housed within the town hall or ruler's palace, in cells constructed wherever space could be found on mezzanines and in attics. Like many other spaces with specific functions, prisons had previously had no separate public indentity. New prisons were more systematically arranged, better ven-

84

85. Antonio da Ponte's New Prisons in Venice (1580s) comprised rooms with specialized functions, such as a torture-chamber, as did Pietro Antonio Barca's prisons in the Palazzo del Capitano di Giustizia in Milan (1578–1636).

tilated, and usually comprised a chapel for prayer, as well as the
standard torture chamber. Those in Venice designed in the
1580s by Da Ponte, provided cells of varying shape, size, and
access to light and fresh air, so that architecturally speaking the
punishment fitted the crime. The prison was also distinguished
as an individual building type with a suitably robust rusticated
façade and iron grills protecting the windows.

The resurgence of interest in the theatre initially prompted
the building of temporary structures and only later its development as a specific building. Ancient examples, such as the
theatre of Marcellus in Rome, were studied and compared
with Vitruvius's text – accompanied in the 1511 edition by Fra
Giovanni Giocondo (1433–1515) with an illustrated reconstruction. Architectural writers were particularly interested in theatres, and Serlio designed a temporary wooden example in the
courtyard of the Palazzo da Porto-Colleone in Vicenza in 1539,
and described and illustrated theatres and stage sets in Book II of
his treatise. Giovanni Battista Bertani (c. 1516–76) designed and
built an *all'antica* semicircular theatre in the Ducal Palace of
Mantua in 1549 and Giulio Camillo composed the important
Idea of the Theatre in 1550; Vasari included a section on academic
theatrical productions in his *Lives*. Architects executed numerous temporary architectural decorations for theatrical performances associated with momentous events such as Charles V's
coronation at Bologna in 1530 and his funeral in 1559 for which
Seregni designed a catafalque. Paul III's entries into Siena in
1538 and 1540 were designed by Bartolommeo Neroni
(c. 1505–71); and Labacco produced decorations for the conclave
that elected Julius III in 1550, and Vignola in 1559 for the conclave of Pius IV. Vasari, Vincenzo Borghini (1515–80) and the
members of the Accademia del Disegno, produced the theatrical
obsequies for Michelangelo's funeral in 1564.

One of the earliest surviving theatres was that designed by
Palladio in 1579–80 for the Olympic Academy of Vicenza. The
elliptical *cavea* and the double height *scenae frons* were directly
inspired by the antique, and sensitively completed by Scamozzi
in 1584. As befitting a theatre for a private academy the Teatro
Olimpico had no public façade, following the tradition of private
theatrical performances held in numerous palace interiors.
Scamozzi, however, subsequently designed the first permanent
public theatre building with an imposing exterior at Sabbioneta,
as part of the urban and architectural renewal of the capital of
this small duchy by Duke Vespasiano Gonzaga (1511–91) from

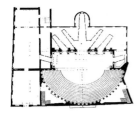

86, 87. Palladio designed the Teatro Olimpico in Vicenza just before his death (1580) and it was completed by Scamozzi (1584). Much of the figurative sculptural decoration was executed by Camillo Mariani who was deeply influenced by the work of Alessandro Vittoria.

the 1550s onwards. The proscenium arch divided the players on stage from the audience in the cavea, and functioned as a framing device for the innovative angular stage sets and perspective scenery. Further innovations in staging theatrical performances included Buontalenti's flat scenes that could be quickly changed to create different illusionistic effects, and the design of scenery that created the effects of great depth and distances by Francesco Salviati (1510–63) and Scipione Chiaramonti (1565–1652). These developments were taken up and extended by Giulio Parigi (1571–1635) who in 1630 also designed the Amphitheatre in the garden of Palazzo Pitti. The other significant scenographer of the period was Aleotti, who was commissioned by Cornelio I Bentivoglio (1519–85) to design the theatre for the Accademia degli Intrepredi in Ferrara in the 1560s. Aleotti also designed the Farnese Theatre in the Palazzo della Pilotta at Parma from 1618–28. The proscenium was the first to have stage wings with wheeled undercarriages that allowed the entire scenery to be changed. For the *cavea* Aleotti employed the double tiered arcade motif of Palladio's Basilica that was greatly influential on subsequent theatre galleries.

175

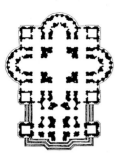

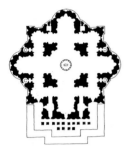

Churches

Churches were located throughout the urban fabric of towns, indicating their integral importance in the daily lives of the inhabitants. Even the smallest villages had a parish church, while large churches stood in the square at every town's heart, and the presence of a cathedral defined a city. The two most important traditional forms, the longitudinal Latin cross, and the centralized church, were seriously reconsidered in both symbolic and practical terms in the light of important liturgical changes, and a return to the traditions of the early Church, as well as the theoretical preferences of architects. The various projects for the rebuilding of St Peter's in Rome, begun by Bramante in 1505 and completed in 1612, illustrate many of these issues.

When Raphael died in 1520, Sangallo was appointed chief architect, together with Peruzzi. While criticizing aspects of his predecessor's design, Sangallo's own proposals retained 88, 90 Raphael's longitudinal form that followed the plan of old St Peter's, whereas Peruzzi experimented with centralized 91 plans. Subsequently, Paul III commissioned another design from Sangallo, but in 1546 Michelangelo abandoned and partially 89

88, 89. Antonio da Sangallo's proposal for St Peter's in Rome comprised a pseudo-longitudinal plan (left above) consisting of a Greek cross with the addition of a nave, Michelangelo (left below) abandoned this in favour of a true Greek-cross.

90. The wooden model of Sangallo's project for St Peter's (opposite) reveals the fussiness of his planned exterior elevation.

91. Peruzzi favoured a sober monumentality for his many centralized plan proposals for St Peter's (right).

92. The exterior of St Peter's as executed by Michelangelo (1550s) is monumental in form: giant order pilasters are surmounted by a substantial entablature and an attic storey punctuated by Michelangelo's unusual window frames.

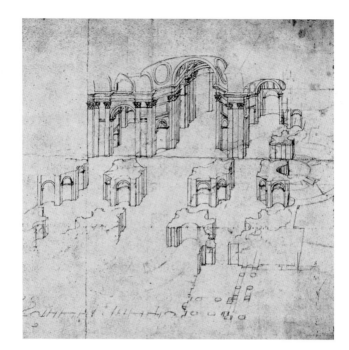

demolished Sangallo's work, stating that 'any who have deviated from Bramante's plan, as Sangallo did, have deviated from the truth'. Michelangelo's own models presented a simplified centralized structure of four strengthened central piers surrounded by an ambulatory and a perimeter wall that was strengthened and transformed into one continuous, colossal structure enclosing the apsidal transepts and chancel that constitute the arms of the Greek-cross plan. The exterior and interior were to be uniformly articulated with giant Corinthian pilasters rising to a prominent entablature surmounted on the interior by a barrel vault and on the exterior with an attic storey. To the east Michelangelo planned a façade of the same order surmounted by

92

93. The interior of Alessi's Santa Maria di Carignano in Genoa (begun 1548) comprises a central crossing, an eight-light drum and cupola, and four barrel-vaulted arms decorated with *all'antica* coffering.

94, 95. The arms of the Greek-
cross plan of Santa Maria di
Carignano are enclosed within
the square body of the building
which has bell-towers in the
corners (only two of the four
were built) and small domes
with lanterns rise over the
four corner chapels.

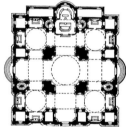

a pedimented portico, but this was not built, and only the drum of
his design for a double-shell dome was executed before his death
in 1564. Della Porta and Fontana built the dome in 1588–91 with
a pointier profile and prominent ribs that provide a strong vertical accent. Michelangelo's vision of a centralized church came to
a decisive end after Paul V Borghese was elected in 1605, and in
1607 ordered Carlo Maderno (1555–1629) to build a nave. This
obstructed the view of the dome from the front of the building,
although it fulfilled the important function of accommodating
large crowds on feast days, and the façade included the benedic-
tion loggia required by papal ritual. For the most important
church of Christendom, practical requirements and tradition
outweighed aesthetic preferences regarding form.

By comparison, when Alessi was commissioned in 1548 to
design the new church of Santa Maria di Carignano in Genoa, he
was able to build a monumental, centralized Greek-cross church

164

93-95

97

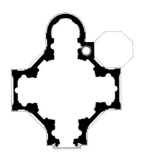

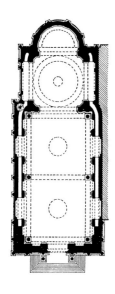

96, 97, 98. The monumental interior of Tibaldi's San Fedele in Milan (begun 1569) culminates with the high altar well lit from windows in the drum of the dome. Tibaldi's first proposal for the Jesuit church (1567) was based on a Greek-cross plan (top), but this was abandoned in favour of the innovative nave articulated with six monumental freestanding columns set on tall pedestals. There are no aisles, but passageways connect the altars in the nave to the chancel.

that summed up the ideals of the period. Bell-towers frame the view of the narrow drum and dome which rise over the central crossing, and the façades are clearly articulated with pilastered bays. The overall clarity of the interior design and articulation is evident in the monochrome treatment of the wall surfaces and the white marble statues in the niches, enhanced by the bright even white light that floods over the central crossing from the drum. Both the arms of the cross and the corner chapels have *all'antica* coffered barrel vaults terminating with thermal windows modelled on those in Roman baths. Alessi's design well represented the spirit of the reformation, officially initiated in 1545 by Paul III, who also founded the Holy Office or Inquisition in the same year, and who summoned the important Council which concluded in Trent in 1563. Paul III aimed to make the church triumphant again through a reformed clergy and Curia, and the Tridentine decrees were approved by Pius IV in 1564, followed by the revised editions of the Roman Breviary in 1568 and the Roman Missal issued in 1570 by Pius V. The decrees of Trent included recommendations regarding sacred art and architecture that were subsequently put into effect and reiterated in treatises such as that on *Sacred and Profane Images* of 1582 by Gabriele Paleotti. One of the most effective ideas was that artists and architects should collaborate with priests who could guide them in creating acceptable work, well represented by Borromeo and Tibaldi's collaboration in Milan.

The most important outcome of the reform was the active encouragement by church leaders such as Borromeo of the New Orders – the great religious phenomenon of the sixteenth century – with the foundation of the Theatines in 1524, the Regular Canons of San Paolo (Barnabites) in 1530, the Somaschi in 1532, the Ursuline nuns in 1535, the Society of Jesus in 1540, and the Oratorians in 1564. Following their official recognition, these orders often embarked on church-building to accommodate their specific needs and practices, and innovative new designs were produced. In Milan, when the Jesuits rebuilt 96-98 San Fedele, the church recently assigned to them, instead of employing the architect of their own order, Giovanni Tristano (d. 1575), Borromeo instead forced Tibaldi upon them. His initial project of 1567 envisaged a centralized church with short projecting arms, but Borromeo persuaded Tibaldi to create a new design in 1569 with a single structural perimeter wall enclosing an aisleless two-bay nave succeeded by a domed sanctuary separated by respondant piers. Six great columns raised

99, 100. The engraving by
Mario Cartaro in Giacomo de
Rossi's *Insignium Romae
Templorum* (1684) shows
Vignola's proposed façade for the
Gesù in Rome (1568). Vignola's
innovative plan (opposite)
comprised a nave without aisles
flanked by deep chapels, linked
by passageways so that the priest
could move between the altars in
these chapels, the altars in the
transept, and the high altar. Four
small domed chapels occupy the
corners beyond the crossing
and can be understood as the
corners of a Greek-cross.

on pedestals support the nave vaults, and frame the articulation
of the shallow altar bays on each flank that are linked by passageways connecting them to the sanctuary. Dispensing with aisles
and chapels enabled Tibaldi to create a single, continuous,
strongly directional interior space, incorporating lateral altars,
succeeded by the sanctuary and high altar – a successful solution
partially repeated by Tibaldi in the 1570s for San Guadenzio at
Novara in Piedmont.

San Fedele was begun just one year after the Jesuit mother
church in Rome, commissioned in 1568 by Cardinal Alessandro
Farnese. Vignola, together with Tristano, developed an earlier
plan of Nanni di Baccio Bigio (which Bigio employed for Santa
Croce at Bosco Marengo near Alessandria in 1567), and devised
an innovative longitudinal plan for the Gesù in which the tradi-

100

101. The façade of the Gesù was built to a new design of Giacomo della Porta (1571) depicted in this engraving by Valérien Regnard, also from de Rossi (1684). The simplicity of the original interior was transformed by sumptuous decoration only in the seventeenth century.

CARDINALI FARNESIO SOC IESV ÆDIFICATI

PARS EXTERIOR *Iacobo de la Porta Architecto* | PARS INTERIOR *Iacobo Barozii a Vignola Architecto*

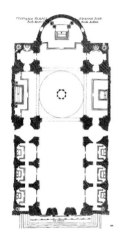

tional three doors of the church all opened into a wide aisleless nave. The nave was flanked by chapels which opened onto it and which were linked by passageways to the short, barrel-vaulted transepts and the apsidal sanctuary to the east. Because the interior was originally only simply decorated, the overwhelming impression was of a single uninterrupted, unified nave space, delimited by the walls articulated with pilasters and entablature and surmounted by a tunnel vault. Beyond the nave the altar was clearly visible, illuminated from the windows in the drum beneath the cupola. Vignola's façade design was, however, passed over by the patron who instead favoured Della Porta's. The difference between the two projects is often considered indicative of a decisive development in architectural design towards a more robust and plastic 'Baroque' conception of the façade, and while this is true, the most significant innovation was Vignola's interior, which indeed symbolized the aims of the reformed church.

99, 101

The Gesù became an influential model for Jesuit churches elsewhere, such as Naples, where Giuseppe Valeriano (1542–96), who had practised architecture in Spain and become a Jesuit

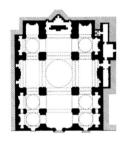

102, 103, 104. The interior of Giuseppe Valeriano's Gesù Nuovo in Naples (1584) is clearly articulated at the crossing with paired pilasters surmounted by a bold entablature. The unusual façade conceals the form of the church laid out on an elongated Greek-cross plan.

there in 1572, designed the Gesù Nuovo in 1584, commissioned by Isabella Feltria della Rovere. Valeriano reused the rusticated façade and some of the walls of the fifteenth-century Palazzo Sanseverino. The Greek-cross plan was elongated by the addition of extra bays on the nave arm that established a longitudinal axial direction within the church. The interior is clearly articulated with coupled pilasters rising to the strong horizontal of the continuous entablature and surmounted by a simple barrel vault. An almost identical plan, with a slightly elongated chancel, was employed by Valeriano for the Jesuit church of Santi Andrea and Ambrogio in Genoa designed in 1589. In 1575 Giovanni De Rosis (1538–1610), a member of the order in Lecce, designed the Gesù there on a Latin-cross plan of great clarity, with an interior brilliantly illuminated by numerous large windows, following his earlier design for the Gesù at Nola in Campania of 1568.

Pioneering churches were also designed in Venice where the original simple white plastered interiors were retained, unlike most churches of the period where later lavish decoration has often been imposed. At San Giorgio Maggiore in 1565, Palladio developed ideas adumbrated by the Benedictines at Santa Giustina in Padua and by Sansovino for San Francesco

103

104

102

105

106

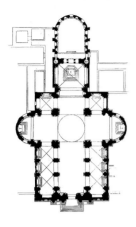

della Vigna, to create a clearly articulated church design. For the Redentore, commissioned in 1576 by the Venetian senate, Palladio synthesized ideas present in Santi Paolo e Barnaba, San Fedele, the Gesù and Genga's San Giovanni Battista at Pesaro for the Franciscans, to achieve a remarkably coherent interior comprising side chapels opening directly from the aisleless nave, and connected by small corridors extending around the sanctuary to provide direct access to the sacristies and choir at the south. Projecting piers with semi-columns demarcate the entrance to the apsidal chancel spaces that act as surrogate transepts, and focus the view from the nave onto the high altar. The four freestanding columns to the south delimit the contiguous spaces of the sanctuary and choir, yet permit light to flood through and illuminate the high altar as the focal point of the interior.

107
108

Related to the reformation programme of church-building was the restoration of Early Christian buildings and a return to their forms in new designs advocated by influential churchmen such as Cesare Baronio (1538–1607). The repair of older structures was undertaken in the 1540s by Giulio Romano at Mantua Cathedral, where he deftly reconciled the medieval parts with his own *all'antica* forms. The enormous dome of the Early Christian church of San Lorenzo in Milan was rebuilt, after it collapsed in 1573, by Bassi, who added structural support for the octagonal entablature below the drumless dome by adding eight large piers, which transformed the interior elevation, but maintained and preserved at the lower level the late antique quatrefoil ground plan. Bassi maintained the character of the original building and yet also provided abundant light from the large windows between the ribs of the dome, as was expected in churches of the period. In Rome, Baronio himself instigated the restoration of the Early Christian churches of Santi Nereo and Achilleo and San Cesareo in 1597 to a form approximating to their original design, an easier task than attempting to complete churches begun in the Gothic style, which faced controversies over the merit of their style. Tibaldi's classicizing work for the interior of Milan Cathedral was highly polemical, and classicizing proposals presented for completing the façade remained resolutely unrealised. At San Petronio in Bologna, the classicizing façade design by Francesco Terribilia (1528–1603) of which only a portion was built, was subsequently demolished despite the approval elicited from Palladio and Martino Longhi the Elder (1534–91).

182

105, 106. The interior of Palladio's San Giorgio Maggiore in Venice (1565) presents a clear white space with light entering from the numerous windows. Flanking the domed crossing are two apsidal transepts and extending beyond it is a separate chancel containing the high altar and a choir for the Benedictine monks.

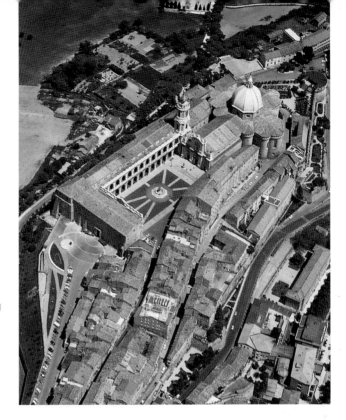

107, 108. The façade of Il Redentore in Venice (designed 1576) is Palladio's most masterful essay in the pedimented temple front flanked by additional segments of temple fronts, here set above a flight of stairs, and executed in crisply carved white Istrian stone. The triconch plan of the sanctuary is inspired by ancient Roman architecture.

109. The approach to the Basilica at Loreto was up a narrow medieval street that opened out into the large square flanked on two sides by the Archibishop's palace and culminating with the façade of the Basilica, designed and built by Giovanni Boccalino, Giovanni Battista Chioldi, and Lattanzio Ventura (1571–87). A series of apsidal chapels surround the domed octagonal crossing and ambulatory.

Another important phenomenon was the building of a spate of pilgrimage churches, from the monumental classicizing Madonna di San Biagio near Montepulciano of 1518, to the renovation in the 1570s of the Basilica of the Santa Casa of Loreto – one of the most important pilgrimage sites in Italy together with the Santo in Padua. At Loreto, the façade was designed in 1571 by Giovanni Boccalini (1520–80) and others and comprised three entrances, to provide access for pilgrims to the aisles that lead to the octagonal ambulatory surrounding the crossing and the Santa Casa, which enabled pilgrims to process through the building. The importance of pilgrimage cannot be underestimated. Pilgrimage was the physical equivalent of the spiritual exercises of Saint Ignatius Loyola (c. 1495–1556) that dominated late sixteenth-century religious life. The great revival of spirituality was achieved by Saint Filippo Neri (1515–95), and Saint Ignatius Loyola who, along with Theresa of Avila (1515–82) and John of the Cross (1542–91) – the two great Spanish saints who reformed the Carmelite Order – represented the extraordinary achievements of the reformed church.

109

Palaces

In the fifteenth century the residential, as distinct from the civic or government, palace usually accommodated a family's commercial activities on the ground floor and their residence on the first and second floors. In a typical palace, the entrance led through to an arcaded central courtyard containing stalls for horses and storage areas, and a wide staircase led from the courtyard to the piano nobile, which contained the rooms where the family lived and received visitors, while the servants were accommodated above them in the attic floor.

In the sixteenth century, as etiquette became increasingly important – as recorded in manuals dedicated to the subject commercial activities disappeared, and the spaces within a palace became increasingly specialized to accommodate a more

110, 111. The Palazzo Farnese in Rome was originally designed by Sangallo (1514) and subsequently expanded and altered in execution by Sangallo (1541), Michelangelo (1546) and others. Rusticated quoins terminate each flank of the façade and rustication is also employed for the entrance, as a prelude to the monumental barrel-vaulted vestibule. On the façade the orders are employed only for the window frames, where they support triangular and curved segmental pediments.

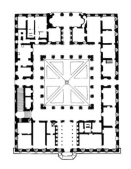

formalized way of living and led to the development of the apartment that comprised a set of rooms to house a single individual such as a cardinal. A cardinal was the model resident of high station for whom treatises such as *De Cardinalatu* of 1510 by Paolo Cortesi were written, but the apartment evolved from a compact set of rooms in the sixteenth century to an enfilade of rooms arranged in a more elaborate sequence by the seventeenth century. Winter suites with low ceilings were often created on the mezzanine floor below the piano nobile, or arranged in parallel with the summer apartments in a wing of a palace, with windows either giving onto the central courtyard or the exterior. Palaces became increasingly monumentalized and began to have a greater variety of small, medium and large rooms, arranged in sequences carefully attuned to ceremonial effect.

The Palazzo Farnese in Rome was greatly enlarged after 1534 by Paul III and set the standard for the sixteenth century. The entrance to the immense freestanding symmetrical block is through a monumental barrel-vaulted vestibule supported by twelve ancient columns leading to the central three-storey arcaded courtyard that provided shelter, enabled circulation, and in this case displayed the Farnese's magnificent collection of antique sculpture. An impressive staircase to the east ascended to the first floor where the visitor traversed the majestic hall westward and entered the apartment designed to house Paul III's son Pierluigi, Duke of Castro. A sequence of rooms, including two anterooms and a chapel, followed the grand *salone* lit by eight windows in the north-eastern corner, and provided ample opportunity for the proper gradations of etiquette to be displayed by the host: how close to the entrance he met his guest, and how far within the apartment the guest was received. The reception of guests and the ordered functioning of the palace depended on the administration of the steward, whose ground-floor office to the right of the entrance was connected to the first floor by a small service stair – indeed the workings of a palace depended on its service stairs that linked public spaces with staff areas such as the *guardaroba* on the top floor that securely housed valuable plate and accommodated the household staff. By the seventeenth century, with an increase in the number and size of apartments, some functions were moved out of palaces to nearby buildings, such as staff quarters for sleeping and eating, as well as the kitchen and pantry that served the palace. Apart from the principal resident housed on the piano nobile, noblewomen of the family had separate apartments with adjacent rooms for

110
111

112

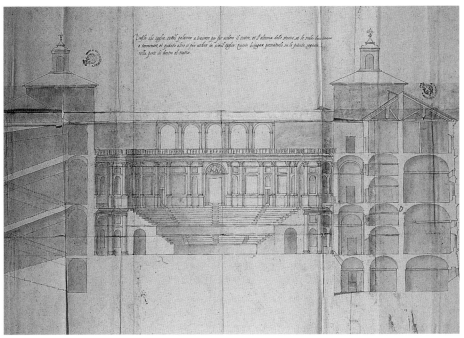

112. The elevation of Sangallo and Michelangelo's courtyard for the Palazzo Farnese in Rome comprises the Doric, Ionic and Corinthian orders. This starkly monumental courtyard originally housed the famed Farnese collection of antique sculpture.

women attendants, in this case on the tall second floor that Michelangelo added and crowned with a monumental cornice. The vast palace was only completed after Paul III's death by his nephew Alessandro, who engaged Della Porta and Vignola to bring to completion the Garden Loggia in 1589, making use of a Papal bull of 1573 enabling the expropriation of adjacent properties. By comparison, Vignola's involvement in the 1558 commission for an extravagantly large Palazzo Farnese in Piacenza was never completed as the project was too grand for the available funds and only a third of the palace was ever built. The most interesting feature of the monumental design was the semicircular *platea* for a permanent theatre planned in the courtyard.

Wealthy Bolognese embarked on many grand palaces in the sixteenth century, including the Palazzo Malvezzi Campeggi of 1522 by Andrea da Formigine (*c.* 1480–1559) who also built the Palazzo Fantuzzi begun in 1525 – perhaps with the involvement of Serlio. The extraordinary façade has rusticated orders and the end bays of the piano nobile display heraldic elephants above the niches – an alternative to the usual display of a family's coat of arms over the entrance. Palazzo Bentivoglio, with its imposing two-storey courtyard was probably designed in 1551 by Bartolomeo Triachini (d. 1587), who also designed Palazzo Malvezzi de' Medici in 1560. The palace of Achille Bocchi was begun in 1545, perhaps to a design by Vignola, and housed the humanist's Hermetana (Hermetic) Academy. All these palaces display an increasing symmetry of design both for the façade articulated by the orders, and the interior arrangement of rooms usually set around one or more courtyards, but these Bolognese palaces remained isolated examples set within the medieval urban fabric of the city.

Quite a different opportunity for palace-building arose with the creation of the via Toledo in Naples in the 1530s, where the adjacent land was razed and then divided into allotments for new building. Patrons and architects took advantage of the regularity of the new street to design symmetrical classicizing palaces with two distinguishing local features: the entrance located on the central axis became the principal focus of the palace façade and developed into a *porte-cochère*, often built at double floor height and given elaborate sculptural decoration, usually executed in the local dark peperino stone. This led through to a large central courtyard where a striking open staircase was developed that enabled access to the numerous floors, including a second piano nobile and often several other floors above, which were a necessi-

113

114

113. Vignola designed a permanent theatre to fill the central courtyard of the Palazzo Farnese in Piacenza (1558) as seen in this original cross-section. A grand public staircase is depicted in the wing to the left of the drawing; to the right low rooms with mezzanines above are flanked towards the courtyard by tall corridors and towards the exterior of the building by wide and spacious full height rooms.

ty given the limited land and great population of Naples (which also made Neapolitan palaces much taller than those in other cities). On the via Toledo examples include the Palazzo Tappia begun in 1528 and expanded in 1566, the palace of the important natural historian Giambattista della Porta begun in 1546, the Palazzo Maddaloni begun in 1582, and the Palazzo Zevallos designed by Cosimo Fanzago (1591–1678) around 1630. Because the via Toledo delimited the eastern edge of the Spanish Quarter, laid out on a classical Roman military grid plan in 1553 and built thereafter, the palaces of some public institutions such as the Conservatory of the Holy Spirit for Poor Girls, begun in 1564, also line the street and served the neighbourhood. In the Spanish Quarter itself slightly smaller plots than those on the via Toledo housed similar palace blocks – in Italian *palazzo* can

114. The unusual façade of the Palazzo Fantuzzi in Bologna (begun 1525), was designed by Andrea Marchesi da Formigine. The smooth and precisely rusticated semi-columns appear delicate and decorative rather than robust, and the thin pilaster strips seem too insubstantial to support the weighty triangular pediments above the piano nobile windows. The sculpted elephant above the niche of the corner bay plays on the name of Francesco Fantuzzi who commissioned the palace.

115. The Palazzo Sanchez-Filomarino (now Giusso) in Naples (begun 1549) was commissioned by Alfonzo Sanchez and later purchased and enlarged (1641) by Ascanio Filomarino, Bishop of Naples, who also commissioned Borromini's only work in the city, the Filomarino altar in the chapel of the Santissima Annunziata at Santi Apostoli (1636). The piano nobile of the sober façade is articulated with Corinthian pilasters that frame each bay in which the principal windows are situated directly on the lower entablature and smaller mezzanine windows just below the principal entablature.

mean single dwelling or a block of residences – but the luxury of the large central courtyard that provided air and sunlight was greatly reduced, if not eliminated altogether, as maximum housing density was a priority. The proportion of courtyard area to residential block in Neapolitan palaces demonstrates the adage than form follows finance.

Form could also be dictated by patrician stature and architectural invention, as in the case of the Vicentine palace commissioned by Girolamo Chiericati in 1549. Because the site was very shallow, Palladio designed a palace with a continuous ground-floor loggia occupying public land, for which a concession had to be issued from the Comune in 1551. Chiericati argued that the loggia would benefit the public as an elegant thoroughfare and benefit himself with extra space for a *salone* flanked by loggias on the piano nobile. Although in plan the flanking wings are three rooms deep, the centre is limited to an apsidal entrance hall, succeeded by a second loggia with double staircases, and a shallow courtyard articulated on the rear wall with the orders and windows as though the palace continued beyond. The openness of the main façade suggested vulnerability and penetrability and was highly unusual, except in Venice where there was a long tradition of open palace façades. Elsewhere architects concentrated their efforts at spatial innovation on the protected interior of the

116
117

palace, and a striking example was the palace of Nicolò Grimaldi in Genoa. Unlike other palaces on the street, that were designed as solid blocks on single lots and only separated by the intervening streets, Grimaldi purchased three contiguous lots on the Strada Nuova enabling him to build a palace that was not only the widest, but freestanding and flanked by gardens raised above street level. The palace entrance is located on the axis of an existing street which ascended from the city below, and the sequential itinerary takes one from the dark vestibule at entrance level containing a staircase which ascends to the large light-filled two

storey arcaded central courtyard. Terminating this courtyard is a monumental double-branch staircase ascending to the upper level of the courtyard and hence by doubling back, to the reception rooms located overlooking the street. Staircases had become a principal feature of palace design, but unlike those in Florentine or Roman palaces, in Genoa they remained open rather than enclosed structures, supported on arcaded loggias suspended in mid-air. In the case of the Palazzo Grimaldi, a further staircase leads to a series of higher terraced gardens at the rear, a route that leads through the various spaces of the palace

113

from dark to light, front to back, and from the lowest to the highest point of the site.

The only comparable palace courtyard was that begun in Rome in 1560 for Tommaso del Giglio, continued from 1586 for Cardinal Pedro Deza who employed Martino Longhi the Elder, and later purchased by Cardinal Camillo Borghese in 1605, just months before he became Paul V. Longhi was a Lombard born in Alessandria (between Milan and Genoa), and the courtyard indeed seems inspired by his experience in the north. By comparison with the ordinary exterior and façade, the rectangular courtyard articulated by a two-storey loggia of arches springing from paired columns is unique in Rome, and contrasts with the irregular block in which it is housed, that was built over a long span of time and incorporated pre-existing structures. The building was completed by Flaminio Ponzio (*c.* 1559–1613) and housed Francesco Borghese, who occupied the eastern portion of the palace. For Giovanni Battista Borghese, a second entrance was built to provide access, via an elliptical staircase, to his new

118. Giovanni and Domenico Ponzello designed and built the Palazzo Grimaldi in Genoa (now Municipio) with a monumental staircase in the entrance hall leading to the central courtyard surrounded by arcaded loggias (1565–79).

apartments that extended to the west of the complex and which were distinctly separate. Paul V's major contribution to the palace, apart from Ponzio's circulation plan that controlled and separated different people moving through the building, was the addition of a hanging garden designed in 1612 by Maderno.

By comparison, Federico Zuccari (1543–1609), who had decorated the façade of his house in Florence with archaeological fragments and rusticated blocks, embarked on a much more ambitious project after his return to Rome in 1588. Gregory XIII Boncompagni (1502–85) had opened the via Gregoriana from Piazza Trinità dei Monte in 1576, and Sixtus V opened the via Felice (later Sistina) in 1586. These projects resulted in a long narrow wedge of land between the two converging streets that Zuccari purchased in 1591 to build his own unusual, four-storey palace that made the best use of the limited site. Because there was a disproportionately high amount of exterior wall surface to interior space, the rooms are well-illuminated by numerous windows, and from the western side one can enjoy spectacular views over Rome. On the ground floor Zuccari located the dining room, bedroom and other practical rooms, while the piano nobile was dedicated to his painting studio at the narrow eastern point and a gallery at the western end overlooking the garden, entered from the street via an unusual portal in the form of a face. However, as etiquette and ceremony became increasingly important, and the linear sequence of the apartment even greater, a site such as Zuccari's would never have been considered by a noble family because of the impossibility of designing a suitably correct sequence of rooms.

Villas

The distinction between a suburban villa such as the Villa Capra-Rotonda and a palace located on the outskirts of town such as the Doria in Genoa is difficult to define, especially as neither had any associated agricultural functions – Palladio significantly placed the Rotonda in the section on palaces rather than villas in his *Quattro Libri*. Essentially, villas were built so that the nobility of a city could escape to their estate in the countryside, where they could relax as well as oversee agricultural production. In the sixteenth century the design of villas became increasingly complex and sophisticated in order to accommodate the various functions of *villeggiatura* – villa life. In Tuscany the traditional compact cubic form of the fifteenth-century villa was transformed through the addition of surrounding terraces,

141

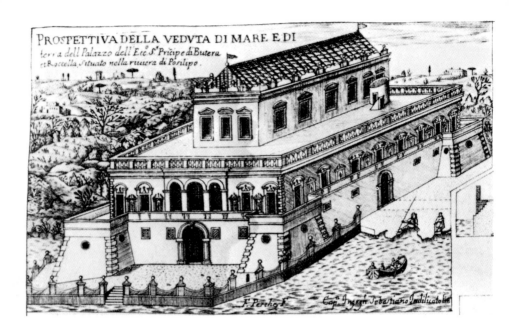

PROSPETTIVA DELLA VEDVTA DI MARE E DI
terra dell Palazzo dell Ecc.o S.r Prícipe di Butera
et Roccella Situato nella riuiera di Posilipo.

119. This engraving of the Villa Carafa di Butera at Posillipo (1588, now destroyed) comes from Biagio Aldimari's *Historia Genealogica della famiglia Carafa* (1691). The villa had a large double-height *salone* reached by a double flight staircase and terminating in a triple loggia affording fine sea views.

and gardens with innovative water games; in the Veneto, the villa complex was a working farm elaborated through the strategy of connecting utilitarian farm buildings to the proprietor's residence to give them an appropriately dignified architectural form; in Lazio ecclesiastical *villeggiatura* led to the creation of magnificent villas of various formal types with extensive fountains and gardens. These developments went hand in hand with architects' exploration of the remains of ancient villas such as Hadrian's, and extensive writing by humanists who sought to recover the ancient culture of villa life written about by Pliny the Younger. A good example was the villa built in 1588 by Fabrizio Carafa, Prince of Butera and della Roccella, by the sea at Posillipo, which seemed to be just one of many attempts at recreating the sort of ancient Roman villas described by Pliny. 119

In Tuscany, the first monumental villas were those built for the Medici at Poggio a Caiano around 1480, and at Castello where the fifteenth-century villa was renovated in 1537 with the addition of fishponds, and an extensive walled garden at the rear that became the model for the Boboli gardens at the Palazzo Pitti. Francesco I commissioned the villa and park of Pratolino from Buontalenti in 1569 to house his mistress Bianca Cappello. The tall but compact block, set upon a monumental podium, overlooked extensive gardens with a series of eight famous grot- 120

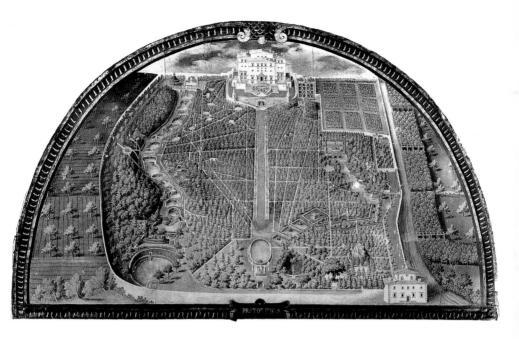

120. Giusto Utens's lunette fresco (1599) depicts Bernardo Buontalenti's Villa Medici at Pratolino (1569).

toes and water games. Visiting Pratolino in the 1580s, Michel de Montaigne sat down on a bench only to discover that it squirted water, the grotto he was in began to flood, and trying to escape provoked further attacks of water ordered by the gardener! Buontalenti designed other villas including Le Marignolle 1587, Castello 1592 and Artimino 1597, and the tradition extended into the seventeenth century when Giulio Parigi, who had added the side wings to the Pitti Palace in 1618, designed the last great Medici villa, Poggio Imperiale, preceded by a grand tree-lined approach built in 1622 for Grand Duchess Maria Magdalena (1587–1629). The Medici villas heralded the development of sophisticated, theatrical gardens in which the pleasure and delight of the visitor was paramount.

Villas in the Veneto were characterized by opposing values and functions. After their defeat at the hands of the League of Cambrai in 1509 Venetians turned their attention to farming in the Veneto as a reliable source of provisions for the city. They pursued the reform of land use and considered its cultivation a sort of 'Holy Agriculture' based on the writing of humanists such as Cornaro. His treatise 'On the sober life' expounded a vision of *otium* dominated by *negotium,* as the escape from the turmoil of city life was to be put to good use by the villa owner who would take healthy exercise and oversee and improve his possessions. Cornaro's Villa dei Vescovi, designed in 1535 with Falconetto, exemplified this vision.

In 1540 the first full romanizing villa was built for Alvise and Girolamo Garzoni at Pontecasale by Sansovino. The monumental two-storey block was set well back from the road, and comprised an enclosed portico leading directly to a Doric atrium which in turn led to the garden beyond. Sansovino incorporated into the scheme for the villa the traditional *barchesse* or storage buildings. They were formally related yet sufficiently detached from the principal residence that was raised on a shallow podium. Sanmicheli employed the same solution for outlying build-

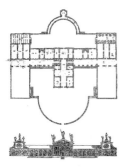

122, 123. The principal reception rooms on the *piano nobile* of Palladio's Villa Barbaro at Maser (late 1550s) are set around a central cruciform-plan hall. Each room is decorated with illusionistic frescoes comprising painted architectural frameworks, mythological and historical figures, and landscapes.

ings at the Villa La Soranza in Castelfranco Treviso of 1540, as did Palladio in whose villa designs it became one of the most notable features. Palladio created a series of innovative villas from the 1540s onwards of which the Villa Emo at Fanzolo, of the late 1550s, combines in an aesthetic unity the principal residence distinguished by the raised portico, and the agricultural buildings set behind series of arcades. Palladio himself described the benefits of this arrangement: 'the cellars, granaries, and stables, and other farm buildings are on either side of the owner's house, and at the ends there are dovecots that are useful for the owner and add beauty to the place; one can move under cover throughout it'. The villa interior was decorated in close collaboration with Palladio by Giambattista Zelotti who executed frescoes of mythological scenes with framing painted columns that appear to support the beams in the ceiling. So too, the interior of the Villa Barbaro at Maser has illusionistic architecture paint-

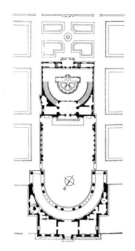

124, 125. The sober
façade of the Villa Giulia in
Rome (begun 1551) designed
by Vignola and others, provides
no hint of the enclosed outdoor
spaces beyond, which include a
Loggia and a sunken Nymphaeum
designed by Ammannati.

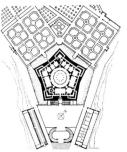

126, 127. Vignola's Palazzo Farnese at Caprarola (begun 1559) dominates the town below, through which the visitor approaches up a narrow street before traversing a sequence of staircases to arrive at the entrance to this massive pentagonal complex.

ed by Paolo Veronese that is closely related to Palladio's architecture. Yet Palladio in his description of the villa never mentioned Veronese's work, and perhaps his collaboration was imposed by the patrons. The Barbaro brothers, Daniele and Marc'Antonio (1518–95), were deeply involved in the design of the villa and Marc'Antonio, who had been Ambassador to Constantinople and then France, personally executed the stucco-work figures for the nymphaeum at the rear of the villa based on models he had seen at Fountainebleau.

The life of humanist retreat for study, relaxation and pleasure that dominated Maser also characterized the Villa Rotonda of 1566. Both patrons were distinguished ecclesiastics: Daniele Barbaro was Patriarch Elect of Aquileia and Paolo Almerico a Monsignor. This type of patronage was unusual in the Veneto, but common in Rome and Lazio where the pope, his cardinals, and their retinues resided. Upon his election in 1550, Julius III commissioned the Villa Giulia from Vignola, who consulted both Ammannati and Vasari, who in turn showed the designs to Michelangelo. At ground level the villa consists of a single suite of three rooms with the central entrance vestibule opening to the hemicycle loggia inspired by Pliny's description of his

128, 129. The innovative circular staircase of the Palazzo Farnese at Caprarola (begun 1559) contrasts architectural membering built of the slightly rough local grey volcanic stone with the delicate *all'antica* frescoes. The same is true of the circular courtyard where classical arches alternate with smaller rectangular openings, enclosing the frescoed loggias.

Laurentine villa. The courtyard terminates with a loggia designed by Ammannati that gives onto a sunken nymphaeum, directly inspired by Genga's Villa Imperiale outside Pesaro. This provided an element of surprise and demonstrated Ammannati's successful integration of architecture and sculpture into the context of the garden. Other villa projects within Rome included the Orti Farnesiani on the Palatine created by Vignola and Del Duca in the 1550s, but most patrons built outside Rome in the Alban hills or at Tivoli, where the splendid gardens of the Villa d'Este were created for Cardinal Ippolito II d'Este of Ferrara in 1559.

The most remarkable hybrid palace-villa was that begun for the Farnese at Caprarola near Viterbo by Peruzzi and Sangallo from 1521. In 1557 Cardinal Alessandro Farnese commissioned Vignola to transform the original pentagonal fortress situated at the end of a long street that bisects the town. The visitor approaching the palace moved off the central axis to ascend one of the paired semicircular ramps to the fortified basement, from where they ascended the double-branch staircase to the ground-floor entrance at the base of the vast palace block. The interior arrangement had two innovative features that were suggested

126
127

by Francesco Paciotto, who modified Vignola's original plans for Caprarola at the request of the patron. The first was the location, well off axis to the left, of the circular staircase that provided access to the sequence of public rooms on the piano nobile. This unusual placement utilized a corner of the pentagonal plan to best effect, and enabled the rooms on the first floor to be set out in a carefully planned sequence adapted for seasonal use and decorated by the finest artists of the day. Shifting the principal staircase away from the centre of the south wing also enabled the ground-floor entrance to give directly onto the double storey circular courtyard located at the heart of the building. This sophisticated courtyard, surrounded by arcaded loggias on both floors, provided a central node for circulation within the building, and its elegant articulation established a striking contrast to the fortress-like character of the exterior, as did the extensive gardens designed by Vignola. The upper gardens and fountains leading to the Palazzina or Casino were designed by Del Duca in the 1580s, and the sunken gardens by Dosio.

Nearby at Bagnaia, Cardinal Gianfrancesco Gambara, Bishop of Viterbo, commissioned a summer retreat in the 1560s

128

129

130. After ascending into the series of garden walkways between the two small casinos of the Villa Lante at Bagnaia near Viterbo (begun 1560s) one encounters the delightful water-chain occupying the pathway on the main axis of the garden. This culminates in a large grotto where the water source for the garden begins its journey along the many channels devised for it before arriving at the splendid fountain in the centre of the formal garden.

131. The Leaning House is just one of the many surprises in the Sacred Wood at Bomarzo near Viterbo (1550s–80s), deliberately built tilting backwards as though it is about to fall over.

132. Della Porta, Carlo Maderno and Giovanni Fontana all contributed to the design of the majestic Villa Aldobrandini (1603–21) set high on the hill overlooking Frascati.

that consisted of two small casinos rather than the traditional single villa. The first casino was executed between 1566 and 1578 by Tommaso Ghinucci (d. 1587), who also created the water displays, and the second was built in 1611 by Maderno for the later owner, Cardinal Montalto. Visitors to the formal garden were able to make their ascent between the two casinos and up the hillside where elaborate sculpted fountains and water games provided entertainment. Bagnaia represents the most genial integration of architecture and landscape where neither dominates but both are perfectly balanced. 130

By contrast, the Sacro Bosco or Sacred Wood of Bomarzo near Viterbo, had no linked residential buildings and was distinctly separate from the patrons' villa located some miles away. It was begun in the 1550s for the military leader Pier Francesco Orsini and built in stages until the 1580s. Here nature predominates over the architecture and sculpture that become episodes within the landscape. The architecture itself presents the idea of the ruin in the form of a Leaning House, a Theatre, a Nymphaeum, and an 'Etruscan' temple and animals that amuse and delight, while the sculptural forms such as the Mouth of Hell 131 are there to astonish and frighten. Wild nature appears to have been briefly tamed in this small oasis with its fountains fed by water from an aqueduct, but the adjacent woods constantly

threaten to overrun it. A greater contrast could not be made between Bomarzo and the recreation of paradise regained suggested by the Villa Borromeo on the Isola Bella at Como, with its lush gardens and island tranquility.

The main region for ecclesiastical *villeggiatura* was east of Rome at Frascati, which was developed in the 1530s by the papal architect Meleghino, during the reign of Paul III. In the second half of the sixteenth century the surrounding area was developed with important villas such as the Mondragone, built for Cardinal Marcus Altemps by Martino Longhi the Elder in 1573 to accommodate Gregory XIII and his court during their frequent visits. From 1603 onwards Della Porta designed a villa for Cardinal Pietro Aldobrandini that dominates the hillside on which it is sited. The land before the tall block of the villa was cleared to allow splendid views over the countryside, whereas there is an extensive wood to the east, separated from the rear of the villa by a nymphaeum designed by Maderno, who completed the villa. The same type of domination was achieved in Rome when Cardinal Ferdinando de' Medici (later Ferdinando I) purchased the villa of Cardinal Giovanni Ricci on the Pincio in 1566 and had it greatly enlarged by Annibale de' Lippi (d. 1581) and Ammannati. The belvederes afford one of the finest views over Rome, and Ferdinando I transformed the villa to include a superb display of antique sculpture on the garden facade that provided the inspiration for many subsequent patrons, including Cardinal Scipione Borghese at his nearby villa. The celebratory display of antique fragments in a building was the equivalent in bricks and mortar of contemporary studies of ancient writing, and symbolized the great importance of the ancient world to the architects and humanists of the late sixteenth century.

Treatises

The renewed interest in ancient writings that discussed architecture focused on the treatise of Vitruvius, and other texts such as Pliny's letters regarding his Tuscan and Laurentine Villas. The first scholarly edition of the *De Architectura* was published in 1511 by Fra Giocondo, and included 140 woodcut illustrations, setting a high standard for subsequent editions, such as the first translation into Italian with commentary by Cesare Cesariano (1476/8–1543) published in folio format in Como in 1521. Cesariano's image of Vitruvian man had greater realism than Giocondo's, and was set within a practical grid from which architectural proportions could be derived; Cesariano was also

132

the first to illustrate the orders as a sequence. Giocondo's and Cesariano's editions were reworked and reprinted by Francesco Lutio Durantino in the 1520s and Giovan Battista Caporali (1476–1560) in the 1530s, and their diffusion made the text accessible both to patrons and architects who read Latin, and to those who did not. Nevertheless, the text remained difficult and in 1558 Giovanni Battista Bertani published a treatise on *The obscure and difficult passages regarding the Ionic Order of Vitruvius,* following his practical demonstration of how the Ionic order was to be constructed by representing it literally on the façade of his house in Mantua in the 1550s.

133, 134. Giovanni Battista Bertani placed these didactic portions of the Ionic order on the façade of his own house in Mantua (1550s) as life-size examples of how to construct the correct proportion and form.

135. Sebastiano Serlio
illustrated the five Orders together
as a sequence on one page of
his treatise (1537). The clarity
of his illustrations made Serlio's
work highly influential.

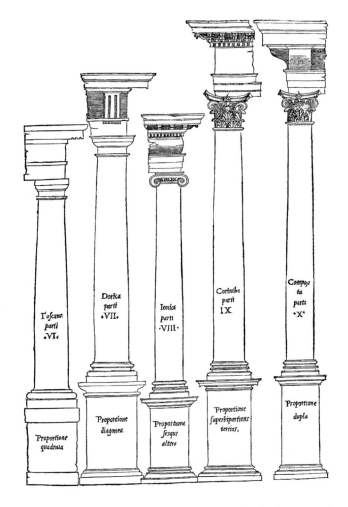

Tofcana
parti
.VI.

Dorica
parti
.VII.

Ionica
parti
·VIII·

Corintha
parti
IX

Compoſi
ta
parti
·X·

Proportione
quadrata

Proportione
diagonea

Proportione
ſeſqui
altero

Proportione
ſuperbipartiens
tertias,

Propottione
dupla

136. Palladio designed the
woodcut illustrations for Daniele
Barbaro's translation of Vitruvius
(1556), including this *scenae
frons* with perspective streets
that closely resembles Palladio's
subsequent design for the Teatro
Olimpico in Vicenza (1579–80).

The difficulties with the Vitruvian text, that had prompted
Alberti to compose his own treatise in the 1450s, were remedied
when a new and reliable translation with commentary was published in 1556 by Daniele Barbaro. Barbaro had worked on his
Vitruvian commentary since 1547, and had made visits to Rome
to study the ancient buildings with Palladio, who provided the
wood-cut illustrations for the treatise. Barbaro, who also published a treatise on *The Practice of Perspective* in 1568, was con-
cerned about the creation of overly rigid rules governing
architectural design, which he believed would result in dull architecture. Instead he suggested architects use their judgement to
design with subtlety and variety, avoiding excessive licence – the
same recommendation of flexibility earlier advocated by mem-

133
134

136

bers of the Accademia della Virtù, founded in Rome in 1542 by Claudio Tolomei (1492–1555), the Bishop of Curzola, that had encouraged Vignola to produce measured drawings of ancient Roman monuments so that the difference between existing monuments and Vitruvius's writing could be examined. Quite the opposite attitude had been taken by Sangallo and his brother Battista (1496–c. 1548), who considered existing translations of Vitruvius inadequate, and had instead undertaken their own. The Sangallo family represented the hardening Vitruvianism of the 1530s and 1540s, and they were dogmatic with respect to the ancient author, using Vitruvian standards not only to criticize contemporaries, but also to inform their own design practice.

However, the increasing appetite for variety and licence was boosted by Serlio who, after working in Rome and his native Bologna, proceeded to Venice where in 1528 he applied for copyright on a series of engravings illustrating the orders. In 1537 he issued the first installment of his treatise, Book IV *On the five styles of building*, in which the Orders are specified as a sequence comprising Tuscan, Doric, Ionic, Corinthian, and Composite, and strikingly illustrated all together on one page, thus codifying them for subsequent use. Serlio's attitude to the past was revealed in Book III, *On Antiquities*, published in 1540: he thought Vitruvius should be respected, although he noted cases where he thought architects might diverge from the ancient author. Serlio's flexibility was demonstrated in the same book through his inclusion of Bramante's Tempietto and Dome project for Saint Peter's, illustrated innovatively with the elevation and section together on one sheet. For Book II, *On Perspective*, and Book I, *On Geometry*, published together in 1545, Serlio used a combination of orthogonal and perspective representation that was deceptively simple and extraordinarily effective, as was Book V, *On Church Building*, published in 1547. In Book IV Serlio had illustrated a number of anticlassical buildings and bizarre fireplaces and in the *Libro Extraordinario* published in 1551 he illustrated a series of licentious portals, along with the statement that, 'most men more often than not enjoy something new', thus reiterating the opinions of Vasari and Barbaro. Collected editions of Serlio's work were published in 1584, 1601, and 1619 thus ensuring his continued influence on architectural design.

It is impossible to underestimate the importance of Serlio's illustrations for the success of his publishing venture. In contrast, the poor images in Pietro Cataneo's *The Four Books* (on the City and Fortifications, Materials, Ecclesiastical Architecture, and Civil and Domestic architecture) published in Venice in 1554, limited its success, and although expanded to eight books in 1567 it was almost immediately overshadowed by two of the most successful treatises ever published, both of which were beautifully illustrated. Vignola's *Rule of the Five Orders of Architecture*, published in 1562, consisted of 32 folio plates mainly illustrating the orders which, together with brief explanatory notes, demonstrated Vignola's rule for establishing the proportion of columns, entablatures, and pedestals according to a module based on the radius of a column and the ratio of the column to the other constituent parts. Vignola offered simple explanations at the bottom of each page, as well as consistent and easily followed ratios that treated all the constituent parts of the orders including pedestal, column, capital and arches, and each of the orders from Tuscan to Corinthian.

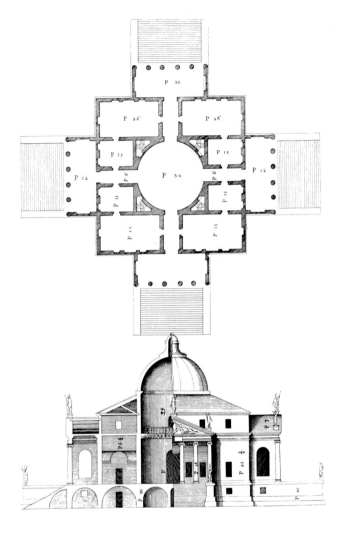

138. One of the most influential woodcut engravings in the entire history of architecture. Palladio's Villa Rotonda on the outskirts of Vicenza, as represented in his *Four Books on Architecture* (1570), included the plan, elevation and section on a single page and inspired many architects and patrons who had not seen the original building.

The other great treatise was Palladio's *Four Books of Architecture* published in 1570, that followed on from his earlier successful publication in 1554 of *The Antiquities of Rome* and *A Description of the Churches, Stations, Indulgences of Rome.* Palladio's chapters comprised: the Materials of Building and the Orders, Country and Town Houses, Public Spaces and Buildings, and Ancient Buildings, and took up many of the themes presented in Barbaro's commentaries to Vitruvius. His attitude towards materials was shaped by Cornaro's treatise that focused on the practicalities and commodiousness of building as well as its economy. Palladio's woodcuts were clear and appealing with the

138

text and image placed on the same or facing pages; and the plan and elevation were placed one above the other so that the idea of the building was immediately conveyed. In addition, the text is clearly written and uses straightforward terminology, thereby proving as useful for the enlightenment of the patron as for the instruction of the architect.

Palladio's treatise was reprinted in 1581, 1601, and 1616 and overshadowed other publishing efforts such as the illustrated translation of Vitruvius by Giovanni Antonio Rusconi (c. 1520–87) only published posthumously in 1590, and Tibaldi's unpublished treatise composed in the 1590s. So too treatises on antiquity by Ligorio and Dosio remained unpublished, as did manuscripts on the Ideal City by Ammannati and Giorgio Vasari the Younger (1562–1625), although the studies of the Milanese Giovanni Battista Montano (1534–1621) were published posthumously in the 1620s and 1630s by his pupil Giambattista Soria (1581–1651). Other successful architectural publications included the *Vestiges of the Antiquities of Rome* published in 1575 by Etienne Dupérac (c. 1525–1604) and the *Treatise on the Art of Painting, Sculpture and Architecture* by Gianpaolo Lomazzo (1538–1600) of 1584. Lomazzo's *Idea of the Temple of Painting* of 1590 presented the practice of art within a philosophical and cosmological context. By comparison, as Principe (Principal) of the Accademia di San Luca, Federico Zuccari's *The Idea of Painters, Sculptors, and Architects*, published in 1607, set out his belief in the importance of the theoretical basis for artistic practice. Zuccari had managed to reform the Academy with the help of Federico Borromeo (1564–1631), and its initial meetings were held in his palace. However, Zuccari's emphasis on design discounted the relevance of a scientific basis for architecture in mathematics.

Architectural theory underpinned by design and grounded in the science of mathematics provided the foundations of the treatise written by Vincenzo Scamozzi who had had a privileged education at the Bishop's Seminary and the Olympic Academy in Vicenza. Scamozzi embarked on an extended study tour south to Naples and then Rome between 1578 and 1580, where he took mathematics classes with Cristoforo Clavio at the Collegio Romano and immersed himself in the study of both ancient and modern buildings. In 1580 Scamozzi published an engraving illustrating his proposed reconstruction of the Baths of Diocletian, and then, in the tradition of Palladio, he published his *Discourses on the Antiquities of Rome* in 1582, comprising

139. Vincenzo Scamozzi's treatise (1615) was a *summa* of sixteenth-century architectural theory as revealed in this image containing references to Leonardo and Michelangelo, as well as displaying Scamozzi's mathematical and geometrical erudition.

forty commentaries to accompany a series of engravings of ancient Roman buildings. Scamozzi also annotated thoroughly Barbaro's Vitruvius, as well as publishing in 1584 a compendium edition of Serlio, which his father Giandomenico (1526–82) had commenced. These works secured his early reputation and demonstrated his profound classical erudition, both textual and architectural, and his ability to incorporate that understanding into his architectural and literary practice through deep knowledge of the ancient and modern sources, which gave him a perfect basis on which to commence the composition of his own magnum opus. Scamozzi's *Idea of Universal Architecture* of 1615 was originally projected in the Vitruvian mould of ten books, of which only six were ever published (just as Gherardo Spini only composed three of his ten projected books on architecture in the 1560s). Scamozzi's treatise is justly considered the last, incomplete, project to represent exhaustively the science of architecture following the Vitruvian model, in which he aimed to cover the whole intellectual and practical spectrum of architectural thought and knowledge.

Together with the numerous treatises published in the sixteenth century, Scamozzi's work stimulated increased recognition of the status and role of the architect. So too, the scientific basis of Scamozzi's treatise paralleled the plethora of treatises published on every subject from stereometry and magnetometry, to perspective and stage design, all of which heralded the creation of the Early Modern world. Yet, another phenomenon of the seventeenth century was the publication of numerous treatises that were more akin to technical manuals, symbolized by the subsequent reduction of Scamozzi's high-flown work full of classical references and modelled on Vitruvius to a glorified builder's manual which focused on the practical issues of construction in later editions and translations. Other works in this genre included the *Information and rules of civil architecture, sculpture, painting, perspective, and military architecture* of 1620 by Giovanni Branca (1571–1640), and the *Architecture* by Gioseffe Viola Zanini 1575/80–1631) published in 1629. Other works focused on limited aspects or details of architecture such as the *Various designs of architectural ornament for doors* by Bernardino Radi (1581–1643) published in 1619. By comparison, a new self-awareness was suggested in the treatise of the philosopher, doctor, and mathematician Teofilo Gallaccini (1564–1641), *On the Errors of Architects*, composed in 1625 and read aloud by its dedicatee Monsignor Giulio Mancini, to Urban VIII Barberini (1568–1644). Although not published until 1767, Gallaccini's self-consciously critical treatise clearly indicated a shift towards a backwards-looking historiographical approach to architectural theory and practice. By contrast, Scamozzi's treatise was still forward-looking and, like Palladio and Vignola before him, Scamozzi was not just a theorist, but also a practitioner of architecture.

Chapter 3: Scamozzi, Maderno and their contemporaries

Venice and the Veneto: Vincenzo Scamozzi

Scamozzi was the most significant architect of his generation, composing a major theoretical treatise and designing a large number of works across a wide range of building types. It was under Scamozzi, and his contemporary in Rome, Carlo Maderno, that two of the great architects of the seventeenth century received their training. When completing the nave interior at St Peter's in the 1620s Maderno's workshop included his nephew Borromini who executed detailed designs for the iron grills under the altars in the crossing. This paved the way for his contribution to the design of the Baldacchino together with Gianlorenzo Bernini (1598–1680) in the last years of Maderno's tenure as chief architect. In Venice, Scamozzi continued construction of Sansovino's Procuratie Nuove, which were brought to completion by Baldassare Longhena (1597–1682) in the 1640s. Longhena had the good fortune of being briefly Scamozzi's pupil and working for him in the final years of his life, when Scamozzi was finishing his treatise.

After training with his father Giandomenico, Scamozzi emerged as an independent architect and was employed to complete a number of buildings left unfinished by his older and much more famous rival Palladio, who died in 1580. The most noted of these was the Villa Rotonda on the edge of Vicenza, for which Scamozzi redesigned and built a shallower cupola in 1581, as well as building the stables. Scamozzi was well qualified for the task, having already designed the Villa Rocca Pisani at Lonigo in 1576, his own variation of the Rotonda. Unlike Palladio's celebrated prototype, which is characterized by its rigorous symmetry of plan and its four identical façades of pedimented porticoes raised above flights of stairs, Scamozzi developed significant variations that enabled him to create a coherent, workable plan that was more functional and comfortable for its inhabitants. This was achieved by placing the interior stairs off the central cross axis and creating smaller and more practical rooms at the rear of the square plan. Externally, the sides and rear of the villa block are architecturally subordinated to the single principal façade, where Scamozzi utilized the portico columns to create a recessed loggia, half indoors and half outdoors, that provided the perfect setting for a summer afternoon in the country. The Rocca Pisani symbolizes both Scamozzi's indebtedness

140. Vincenzo Scamozzi's Rocca Pisani at Lonigo (1576) is set on the top of the hill and affords fine views of the surrounding countryside. The steep, unrelieved ascent to the Rocca was unusual among villas of the Veneto, and approaching in a carriage must have been a notable experience. Whereas the pedimented porticoes of the Rotonda project out from the block of the villa, Scamozzi enclosed the single loggia of the Rocca Pisani within the block to create an indoor-outdoor space that is wholly integrated into the villa building, following Palladio's example at the Villa Emo at Fanzolo (late 1550s).

141

140

138

141. The Villa Rotonda by Palladio on the outskirts of Vicenza (begun 1566) is the most atypical of Palladio's villas but also the most famous and influential because of its abstract compositional perfection, actually an assemblage of various elements never used before in villa architecture – most notably the cupola.

to Palladio, and his subtle attempt to improve upon the Palladian model with variations that reveal his profound consideration of function and planning. The minimal use of the orders and the austere decoration of both interior and exterior are evidence of an aesthetic that anticipates the taste of two centuries hence. By contrast, Scamozzi created a very different display of austerity for Pietro Duodo who, after receiving authorization in 1605 from Paul V, commissioned the recreation in microcosm of the seven pilgrimage churches of Rome along the approach to his villa at Monselice designed in 1592. The path to the villa took the visitor past each of the chapels, in an overt and rhetorical display of reformation piety that was far removed from the atmosphere of the Rocca Pisani, the Villa Rotonda, and even the Villa Barbaro, where Palladio's Tempietto was sited below and away from the residence.

The issue of siting buildings became increasingly important in the late sixteenth century as patrons aimed to achieve ever more conspicuous results. At Monselice, because the chapels are located prominently along the hillside, they were visible from a great distance. So too in Venice, patrons exploited the visibility of sites wherever possible, and palace façades became increasingly lavish architectural displays, especially on the prestigious Grand Canal, the city's main thoroughfare. In 1582 Nicolò Balbi commissioned Alessandro Vittoria (1525–1608) to design him a palace on a major turning point known as the 'Volta del Canal' and the finishing point of an annual regatta. Vittoria fully

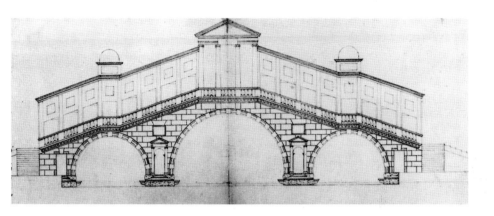

142. The 'Bridge of Sighs' is a purely Romantic invention, although Antonio Contin's design (1600) did serve the practical purpose of providing connecting passageways between the Ducal Palace and the New Prisons of Venice.

143. Scamozzi's proposal for the Rialto Bridge (1587) situated half way along the Grand Canal in Venice, comprised three round-headed arches that would have provided sound structural support but which restricted the size of vessels that could pass underneath.

exploited the location to create an elaborate façade that functions almost as a backdrop to the theatrical space of the canal, and that could be seen from far away at the Scuola della Carità (now the Accademia) and at the Rialto.

Rebuilding the Rialto bridge presented another good visual opportunity that Scamozzi's design of 1587 fully exploited to create an impressive monumental structure that carefully channelled movement across the bridge in a way that increased its inherent theatricality. Unlike the original bridge and Palladio's two proposed reconstructions, which envisaged enclosed spaces traversing the Grand Canal, Scamozzi's project offered a completely different approach to public space through the provision of two flights of stairs flanking the central gradient, from which people crossing the bridge could see and be seen along the Grand Canal. Scamozzi proposed a structure of three round-headed Roman arches justified, in a written memorial, by reference to the treatises of Vitruvius and Alberti, but his design was rejected in favour of Da Ponte's single span project of 1588. Scamozzi retaliated with another proposal that incorporated elements from the first project into a single arch design very close to the bridge as built, making Scamozzi's involvement there difficult to evaluate. In fact, the Venetian authorities usually asked several architects to submit designs for a project, from which they chose the best features and employed a competent

144. The innovative planning of Scamozzi's Palazzo Contarini degli Scrigni (begun 1609) broke with Venetian tradition by locating a large reception room along the façade. This is reflected in the equal spacing of the windows, rather than the traditional grouping of three or more lights in the centre of the façade.

engineer such as Da Ponte to incorporate them into his own project. Scamozzi's external flights of stairs recognized the public and ceremonial aspects of the bridge's function – quite the opposite of the Bridge of Sighs designed by Antonio Contin 142 (1566–1600) at the end of his life and built from 1600, to connect the Ducal Palace to the Prisons built in the 1580s, and from which Giacomo Casanova later escaped.

Scamozzi's reverence for the fundamental tenets of romanizing classical design impeded his success in Venice where the government preferred the practical approach and technical expertise of an architect and foreman of works who would execute the wishes of the patron. For example, Da Ponte had been appointed in preference even to Palladio to superintend the Ducal Palace in 1554, and was therefore responsible for supervising its reconstruction after the two fires in the 1570s. Scamozzi did, however, receive the opportunity to work on a major public project in the 1580s, when he was employed to bring to completion Sansovino's Library and the Procuratie Nuove. Scamozzi's proposal to add a third storey to both buildings was rejected for the Library because of its proximity to the Ducal Palace, but accepted in the case of Procuratie Nuove because it provided much needed additional accommodation. Scamozzi's third storey also established a harmonious proportion of height to length along the south side of Piazza San Marco, in the same way as the two-storey Palazzo della Gran Guardia in Verona was sensitively designed in 1609 by Sanmicheli's nephew Domenico Curtoni (1556–c. 1627) to create a harmoniously proportioned building for the large piazza in front of the ancient arena.

The Teatro Olimpico was also completed by Scamozzi, who 86, 87 designed the innovative perspectival stage sets to recreate the seven avenues of Thebes required for the inaugural performance of 1585 when Sophocles' *Oedipus Rex* was performed in Italian translation. Scamozzi's receding avenues were carefully based on a woodcut reconstruction of an ancient theatre that Palladio had designed for Barbaro's edition of Vitruvius – Scamozzi owned and extensively annotated his copy of the second edition of Barbaro. Scamozzi subsequently had the opportunity to further explore his interest in theatre design when, in 1588, the 173 architectural enthusiast Duke Vespasiano Gonzaga commis- 174 sioned a theatre as one of a series of new buildings needed to complete the capital of his small duchy at Sabbioneta near Mantua in Lombardy.

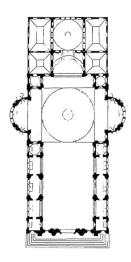

Scamozzi received a number of commissions for churches and conventual buildings from religious orders such as the Celestine nuns in Venice, for whom Palladio had built the cloister in the 1570s. In 1582 Scamozzi was asked to design their church, and he created an overtly romanizing design for Santa Maria della Celestia that was directly based on the Pantheon – a misguided choice for an order of nuns in the context of reformation Venice, a city where Rome was always regarded with suspicion. Construction was halted after a few years and the building abandoned for a further twenty years leading one of the Celestine nuns to describe it as a 'monster of architecture – a body without its head'. It was finally demolished and replaced with a conventional design by another architect in 1605, the same year that Venice was placed under Interdict and excommunicated by Paul V. This unfortunate episode demonstrated the conflict that could occur between architects who wanted to build something of their own design, and the ultimate authority of the patron who paid for the building. The nuns must have hated the church a great deal to undertake the extravagantly expensive demolition and rebuilding programme. The incident also tangentially illustrates Scamozzi's scathing adage – found in his treatise – that tasteless patrons always build badly – or in this case that patrons who do not really know what they want are bound to be disappointed. It is inconceivable that Scamozzi had not shown the nuns preparatory drawings. Either they simply hadn't understood the meaning of the proposal or had changed their minds after building work began.

In 1581 Scamozzi was commissioned by the Theatines – the New Order founded by Gaetano Thiene (1480–1547) – to design and build their church in Padua. There Scamozzi carefully reconciled his aesthetic preference for a centralized plan rising to a cupola and oculus with the need to provide a clearly directional interior, achieved by adding a chancel and choir beyond the lay space of the central octagon. For the Theatines in Venice, however, Scamozzi's brilliant design for San Nicolò da Tolentino of 1591 was again overshadowed by problems during construction and he was dismissed. Yet his wide, aisleless nave flanked by chapels and succeeded by a crossing, with short apsidal transepts, and a chancel and choir, clearly demarcated individual spaces within the interior and established a hierarchy between them, thus ensuring the focus remained on the high altar. Each of Scamozzi's churches for the New Orders was different because designs that satisfied the new post-Tridentine

145

liturgical requirements were still being developed and tested both by architects and the Orders. Increasingly the Orders looked among their own members for architects who could ensure a satisfactorily designed building and promulgate the use of these approved models by travelling throughout Italy and building churches for their Orders.

The Spanish-ruled South

After 1503 all of Southern Italy below the Papal States and Rome was known as the Kingdom of the Two Sicilies and governed by Habsburg-appointed Viceroys. There was a huge increase in the population of cities such as Bari, Capua, and especially Lecce which almost doubled the number of its inhabitants, and new buildings of all sorts were required. Despite Spanish rule, much of the architecture and sculpture of the period was executed by artists from Central and Northern Italy who had travelled to find work or fulfill commissions for the leading patrons: the Viceroys with their building programmes, and the New Orders which required churches and conventual buildings. In Naples these works of urban renewal were initiated by Don Pedro of Toledo, Viceroy 1532–1553, while in Palermo successive Viceroys from Ferrante Gonzaga 1535–46 and Juan de Vega 1547–57 onwards instigated the building of new city walls designed initially by Antonio Ferramolino (c. 1495–1550). Later significant projects included the creation of the Piazza Pretoria in 1574 by Camillo Camilliani (d. 1603) with its impressively reconstructed fountain by his father Francesco (c. 1530–86). The adjacent thoroughfare of the Cassaro or via Toledo, established in the 1560s and largely executed by Giuseppe Spadafora (d. 1572), terminated with the city gates of the Porta Felice and 146 Porta Nuova of 1582–83 built for Viceroy Marc'Antonio Colonna who ruled 1577–84. The Cassaro, and the Via Maqueda built in the 1590s, together established the urban heart of Palermo at the crossroads known as the Quattro Canti with its four palaces and fountains. Religious Orders such as the Jesuits took advantage of the new road and built their Collegio 147 Massimo there in 1586, expanding beyond their first church, the Gesù, designed in 1564 on a Latin-cross plan with a single nave and cupola by the Jesuit, Tristano of Ferrara. Private patrons also built impressive palaces along the Cassaro, such as Giacomo Castrone who in the early 1560s commissioned the tall three-storey Palazzo Castrone-Santa Ninfa whose giant 148 order pilasters create a façade of strong vertical articulation, and whose Michelangelesque pedimented windows extend across the façade and along the side walls of the palace.

The Viceroys not only renewed the capital, but undertook the defence of the island as a whole, employing architects such as Giunti of Prato, who supervised the construction of fortifications along the Sicilian coastline from the 1540s onwards, and Camillo Camilliani, who wrote an important report on coastline defences in 1574. In Messina, the fortified coastal city closest to the Italian mainland, the local architect Francesco La Cameola constructed the first civic aqueduct from 1530–47 that terminated in front of the cathedral with its two classicizing fountains dedicated to Orion (1547) and Neptune (1553), which were executed by the Tuscan servite friar, Giovanni Angelo Montorsoli (1507–63), who had earlier worked on Michelangelo's New Sacristy. The cathedral square was connected with the Royal Palace by the via Austria built in the 1570s, and in the 1580s the strada Colonna that provided a second major thoroughfare in the city.

In 1548 the first Jesuit college in Sicily was established in Messina, followed by the other Orders who built numerous churches, including San Giovanni di Malta by Giacomo del Duca. Del Duca was a Sicilian from Cefalù who trained with the local Gagini masters before transferring to Rome, where he became Michelangelo's principal assistant; he later designed the

146. The Porta Felice in Palermo (1582–83), possibly designed by Giovan Battista Collepietra and others, was erected for Marcantonio Colonna and provides a magnificent entrance to the city with its pairs of great columns set on tall pedestals and supporting massive entablatures.

147. The Collegio Massimo in Palermo (1586) exhibits a sober classicism appropriate for the members of a religious order. The adjacent church of Santa Maria della Grotta was built later (1615).

149

boldly ribbed cupola and elaborate lantern of Santa Maria di Loreto in Rome, in 1573. San Giovanni di Malta was built shortly after his arrival in Messina in 1588, and its remarkable façade articulated by clusters of overlapping giant order Doric pilasters established a new current of romanizing architecture in Sicily. A good indication of the interest in architectural theory was demonstrated by Del Duca's commis-sion from the Jesuits of Messina to write a treatise modelled on Alberti's.

On the mainland, Giovanni Tarantino (d. 1603) designed in 1576 the impressive church of San Domenico at Nardò near Lecce. Lecce itself flourished under Spanish domination with the construction of new city walls, an enormous fortress, and a hospital rebuilt in 1548 by Gian Giacomo d'Acaia (active 1530–70) which was administered by the commune as a civic hospital, and where the systematic planning provided specialized rooms for different functions. The New Orders, which were then undertaking extensive building campaigns throughout the peninsula,

149. Giacomo del Duca's design for the church of San Giovanni di Malta in Messina (1588) employed Michelangelesque giant pilasters to create a robust and monumental exterior (later damaged by earthquake).

constructed important and innovative churches and conventual buildings in Lecce. For the Celestine Nuns of Santa Croce, Gabriele Riccardi (1528–*c.* 86) designed in 1549 a Latin-cross church of Brunelleschian inspiration and clarity, to which a lower façade with powerfully projecting columns was added by Francesco Antonio Zimbalo (active 1567–1615) in 1606. In 1575, a member of the Jesuit order, Giovanni De Rosis from Comasco, designed the Gesù on a Latin-cross plan and provided brilliant illumination for the interior through the provision of numerous large windows in the clerestory. The use of a company architect exemplifies the decision taken by the Jesuits in 1564 that all building projects were to be approved by the General of the Jesuit Order. This decree was aimed at obtaining church designs that were consistent with the needs of the Order, and was aided in execution by having members of the Company who practised architecture, such as Tristano who began the Gesù Vecchio in Naples 1558–62, which was completed by Pietro Provedi (1562–1623) after 1614.

150

The Theatines likewise employed their own member and architect, Francesco Grimaldi (1543–*c.* 1613), to produce plans

150. Santa Croce at Lecce was designed for the Celestine Nuns in 1549 by local Gabriele Riccardi (active 1524–c. 1582); the lower façade was designed by Francesco Antonio Zimbalo (1567–c. 1615) of Lecce in 1606 and the upper façade of 1646 by Giuseppe Zimbalo, executed by Cesare Penna.

and models in the early 1590s for Sant' Irene in Lecce, which explains the presence of a church based on recent Roman models in a city where a strong local style was then developing. Apart from a Roman sojourn in 1591 to contribute to the design of Sant'Andrea della Valle, Grimaldi lived and worked in Naples. There the building campaigns of the New Orders were transforming the city – one of only two in Europe that had a population of more than 200,000 (the other was Paris). Viceregal legislation enacted after the Council of Trent favoured the clergy, and inaugurated an innovative phase of religious building characterized by the work of architects such as Grimaldi, who designed San Paolo Maggiore for the Theatines in 1583, and his masterpiece, Santa Maria degli Angeli a Pizzofalcone of 1600, where the majestic design of the church comprises a long nave, 151 separated from the aisles by four boldly articulated arches, and surmounted by a barrel vault succeeded by a powerful drum and dome. This innovative church, together with Grimaldi's Santi Apostoli of 1609, represents a high note of Neapolitan ecclesiastical design.

The prominent Florentine architect Giovan Antonio Dosio came to Naples in 1590 after working in Rome in the 1550s and 1560s, and in Florence from 1576 where he designed a model for the façade of Florence cathedral. Dosio, like Montano after him, was a highly skilled draughtsman who produced numerous drawings of his immediate predecessors' and contemporaries' work, and also of antique architecture. Dosio's draughting skills had already enabled him to work increasingly in a collaborative or supervisory role for projects both in Florence and further afield including Padua and Rome, by furnishing designs that were executed by others. In Naples, with Father Antonio Talpa the Rector of the Oratorian Congregation, Dosio revised the design of the Girolamini which had been begun in 1587 by his compatriot Dionisio di Bartolomeo Nencioni (1559–1638). The Brunelleschian plan, with freestanding marble columns supporting the nave arcade indicated the return to Early Christian schema favoured in the reformation and in particular by the Oratorians, founded by Filippo Neri and officially recognized in 1590. Dosio held the post of Royal architect and engineer 1593–96, and worked on several projects including the Certosa of San Martino above Naples, where he probably designed the large cloister with its Brunelleschian perspectival effects along each range.

In response to the steep terrain of the city, architects building churches in Naples designed tall flights of stairs to connect the street level with the raised exterior entrance vestibule, which usually comprised a deep three-bayed portico often forming the lower floor of the church façade proper. An innovative and influential plan was developed at San Gregorio Armeno in 1574 by Cavagna who designed a single nave flanked directly by chapels but preceded by a second choir, located above the entrance vestibule, that responded to the needs of female enclo-

151. Francesco Grimaldi designed a solemn, majestic interior for Santa Maria degli Angeli a Pizzofalcone in Naples (1600) with clusters of overlapping pilasters in the nave and crossing. The high altar is clearly visible throughout the nave.

sure. This model was taken up by Giovan Giacomo Conforto (*c.* 1569–1631) at Santi Marcellino and Festo in 1626, where the simply designed architecture supports a rich interior decorative ensemble, and also by Cosimo Fanzago of Bergamo, whose innovative designs included the Ascensione at Chiaia begun in 1622. Many church interiors were sumptuously decorated in a magnificent combination of marble, gilding and stucco, yet a second tendency towards the austerity that had characterized churches such as Santa Maria Donnaromita, designed in 1535 by Giovanni Mormanno, also thrived and was taken up by the Dominican Fra Giuseppe Nuvolo (1570–1637) in the church of Santa Maria della Sanità designed in 1588, and by Conforto at Santa Maria della Verità of 1612 where the interior is dominated by white stuccowork and brilliantly illuminated with light. Nuvolo's preference for monochrome interiors certainly helped the appreciation of his innovative plans, whereas rich colour or decoration would have rendered them incomprehensible, particularly his original proposal for Santa Maria della Sanità which included an octagonal sacristy and an oval cloister.

Ecclesiastical building has survived the ravages of successive earthquakes much better than secular buildings, which have also suffered from additions and modifications as taste and practical requirements have altered them – often beyond recognition. However, a good example of noble Neapolitan patronage is represented by the Palazzo Carafa di Montorio, commissioned in 1559 by Alfonso Carafa, whose uncle Gian Pietro, a founder of the Theatine Order, had become Paul IV in 1555. Upon being raised to the purple Carafa had commissioned his compatriot Ligorio to design the Casino in the Vatican Gardens, while another member of the family, Prince Fabrizio Carafa, subsequently built a villa at Posillipo in 1588 comprising a bastioned basement, a large hall on the piano nobile that was lit by clerestory windows and a loggia, and a roof terrace that provided stunning views of the sea below. The Carafas also commissioned Dosio in 1598 to renovate the Capella Brancaccio in the Cathedral as a mausoleum befitting their status as a papal family.

It was the death of another pope, Sixtus V, in 1590 that provided the impetus for the arrival in Naples of Domenico Fontana, who had designed the pope's catafalque in Rome before being effectively exiled, without hope of further commissions after the death of his most important patron. In 1592 Fontana accepted the invitation of Viceroy Conte di Miranda 1586–95 and designed the church of Gesù and Maria in 1593–1603 before

153
152

152. Giovanni Giacomo di Conforti built Santa Maria della Verità (1603–27) with a monumental barrel-vaulted nave and chancel and a brightly lit crossing. The church was restored in 1688 and again in the eighteenth century, but remains one of the most important examples of seventeenth-century Neapolitan art and architecture, including paintings, stuccoes and marbles.

153. Fra Nuvolo's design for the church and convent of Santa Maria della Sanità in Naples (1588), as recorded in the engraving by Fra Angelo Maiorino, comprised an unusual centralized church with multiple apsidal chapels lining the perimeter, and an adjacent oval cloister. The church was eventually built (1602–13) on a traditional Latin-cross plan, with a brilliant white interior and an innovative staircase leading to the raised chancel.

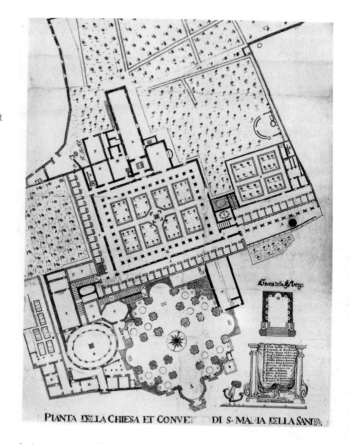

PIANTA DELLA CHIESA ET CONVEI DI S· MA·IA DELLA SANTA

being appointed Royal Architect in 1596, succeeding Dosio. His most important commission came from Viceroy Francisco de Castro 1601–03, who in 1601 ordered the construction of the immense Royal Palace that was built under the supervision of Fontana's son Giulio Cesare (1580–1627) his successor as Royal Architect in 1607. In 1611, for Viceroy Pedro Fernandez de Castro 1610–16, Giulio Cesare designed the Palazzo dei Regi Studi of the university (now the Archaeological Museum), transforming the existing single-storey stables into a two-storey complex with two large courtyards separated by a long central arcade terminating with a hemicycle for literary orations. Cesare's collaborator at the Royal Palace, Bartolomeo Picchiatti (c. 1571–1643) of Ferrara, succeeded him in 1627 as Royal Architect and saw to completion the enormous building which included two floors of public reception rooms above the original portico of twenty-one continuous arcades, providing the type of lengthy enfilade of rooms required for rulers.

154

At the beginning of the seventeenth century in Sicily the informed and sophisticated architectural milieu on the island was well represented by three notable buildings. One was the Corte Capitaniale at Caltagirone designed in 1601 by Antonuzzo Gagini (d. 1627) and built by Domenico Gagini. This long single-storey building that housed the local magistrates has an innovative plan and a genial façade with an elegant sequence of doors and windows set above a scenographic approach staircase created as part of a new urban axis designed by Giuseppe Giacalone (active 1564–1608). Giulio Lasso, who went on to design the monumental façades of the Quattro Canti in Palermo, designed the majestic marble-columned cloister of the Benedictine convent of San Nicolò l'Arena in Catania in 1608. In the same year Natale Masuccio designed the cathedral at Milazzo, and also the fine classicizing portal for the Jesuit college in Messina, where the most extraordinary building project, the Palazzata along the shoreline, was begun in the 1620s but destroyed in the earthquake of 1908

155

The Rome of Della Porta and Maderno

Reformation Rome was characterized by the Neapolitan Paul IV elected in 1555, who helped found the Theatine Order; Pius IV elected in 1559, who commissioned Santa Maria degli Angeli from Michelangelo; and the saintly if puritan Dominican Pius V elected in 1566, who had the antique statues removed from the Vatican Belvedere. A more enthusiastic era was ushered in during the pontificate of the Bolognese Gregory XIII elected in 1572, who exploited the opportunity provided by the Holy Year of 1575 to effectively carry out urban reform and to instigate new building work.

In 1574 Gregory XIII issued a bull codifying aspects of planning that gave greater power to the office of the *maestri delle strade*, which was reorganized, and which redefined the law relating to public thoroughfares and the private dwellings that lined them, enabling the widening of existing streets and the construction of new ones such as the via Merulana and the via Gregoriana. Gregory XIII gave important recognition to religious institutions such as Saint Filippo Neri's Oratory, which took up its new home at Santa Maria in Vallicella, rebuilt under 156 the influence of its prefect Father Talpa by the Oratorian Giovanni Battista Guerra with a façade designed in 1593 by Fausto Rughesi. Gregory XIII promoted the establishment of the Jesuit Collegio Romano in 1582 as part of the teaching mis-

sion of Loyola's Society of Jesus, yet he also understood the importance of art and architecture and gave official recognition to the Academy of Saint Luke, established under the direction of its first *principe* Federico Zuccari; he donated the church of Santa Martina to the Academy, which Pietro da Cortona (1597–1669) would rebuild from 1634. Gregory XIII's first appointment as papal architect was the Lombard Martino Longhi the Elder who built the Villa Mondragone at Frascati in 1573 and the Palazzo Altemps in Rome in 1575, but Longhi's bland conformist style led to his replacement in 1577 by the brilliant Ottaviano Mascherino (1536–1606), a Bolognese who arrived in Rome in 1574. At the Vatican Mascherino built the Gallery of the Maps and the Tower of the Winds, and on the Quirinale hill began construction of the pope's summer residence, which eventually included a huge urban courtyard for receiving guests, and Mascherino's innovative and highly influential oval staircase of 1577 with its paired Doric columns.

Gregory XIII's bull of 1574 was employed vigorously by his successor, the reforming Franciscan Sixtus V, who was elected in 1585 and immediately decreed an extraordinary Jubilee year. In 1586 he issued the bull regarding building and restoration: *Roma Sancta Renovata*, which set out his vision of a restored and tri-

157

umphant Christian Rome based on a return to the liturgy of the Early Church and a revival of processions to the seven pilgrimage churches along streets such as the Via Felice that connected Trinità dei Monti with Santa Maria Maggiore and Santa Croce in Gerusalemme. In 1588 Sixtus V also instigated the transformation by Matteo Castello (1525–1616) and Giovanni Fontana (1540–1616) of Alexander Severus's ancient aqueduct into the Acqua Felice, which terminated with a triumphal arch and fountain adjacent to the Baths of Diocletian and the church of Santa

158. It was Domenica Fontana's technological expertise that enabled him to move the Vatican obelisk into position without breaking it (1586). The great wooden cradle he employed was recorded in Fontana's celebratory book, *Della trasportatione dell'obelisco vaticano* (1590).

Susanna, which Sixtus V's sister Camilla Peretti patronized in its first phase of renovation. The via Felice, together with the via Pia, created the central crossroads of the Quattro Fontane named after the fountains set within the corner niches, containing statues representing the rivers Tiber and Arno, and the goddesses Diana and Juno, executed 1588–93. Sixtus V's most famous commission – to transfer and re-erect the Vatican obelisk in front of St Peter's – was awarded in 1586 to Domenico Fontana who designed a pyramidal wooden machine that cradled the obelisk 158 and enabled it to be slowly lowered, moved and raised aloft in its new position without breaking. This great technical achievement became a highly celebrated event and was recorded in Fontana's own commemorative book of 1590 that explained the technicalities of *The Transportation of the Vatican Obelisk*. Fontana, whom Sixtus V made a knight of the Golden Fleece for his achievement, subsequently set up other obelisks on the Esquiline at Santa Maria Maggiore 1587, at Santa Maria del Popolo 1589, and at San Giovanni in Laterano 1585–89, all three with the help of his nephew Maderno whom Fontana introduced to future patrons, just as Maderno would later promote Borromini. For Sixtus V, Fontana also designed the Vatican Library in 1587 and restructured the Scala Santa in 1588, but the limit of his architectural talent was exceeded with the 1585 commission to design the Lateran Palace, whose stolid aspect was exacerbated by the repetitious windows on its monotonous façades.

In this period, when architects had more practical and technical skills than theoretical or architectural talent, the skill and flair of Della Porta stood out. Together with Fontana he was responsible for the construction in the late 1580s of the enormous dome of St Peter's with its great internal span. Making use of the enhanced structural capabilities provided by the patented brick-making process developed in 1551 by Baccio Bigio, Della Porta and Fontana demonstrated how expertly trained practitioners of architecture and engineering could vault such an enormous area, while avoiding the structural errors so often made by those trained as sculptors, such as the doomed bell-towers of St Peter's begun in 1637 by Gianlorenzo Bernini. Apart from his work at St Peter's, in 1564 Della Porta had succeeded Michelangelo as architect of the Roman people and he pursued the construction of the palaces on the Capitoline Hill; he was also in charge of the Cardinal's congregation for roads, bridges, and fountains, and influenced the process of urban renewal in his advisory capacity. His own capabilities as a designer were made

159. Giacomo della Porta designed a wide, spacious nave for the Theatine church of Sant' Andrea della Valle in Rome (1591).

clear when his proposal for the façade of the Gesù was chosen in preference to that of Vignola, whom he succeeded as architect of St Peter's in 1573. Della Porta designed numerous Roman churches of distinction including Santa Maria ai Monti, Sant'Anastasio dei Greci, and San Luigi dei Francesi in 1580; and the façades of Santa Catarina dei Funari in 1564 and San Nicola in Carcere in 1599. In 1591 Della Porta was also involved in the design of Sant' Andrea della Valle, revising in collaboration with Pietro Olivieri (1551–99) the plans furnished by Grimaldi, who had won the official competition to design the church. As it was originally outfitted, the church had a plain, barrel-vaulted nave leading to a drum and dome over the crossing and an apsidal chancel, all of which appear linked in the expansive and unified space of the longitudinal interior, and enclosed by the clustered masses of pilasters framing the arched chapel openings and the monumental entablature above. In contrast, in San Salvatore in Lauro, designed in 1591, the nave space seems constricted and

159

160

contained by the powerful pairs of giant columns, and divided into sections by the projections of the broken entablature and the triumphal arches that define the crossing.

Apart from large preaching churches, a number of smaller churches with a variety of innovative plans were built, including the oval plan of San Giacomo in Augusta at the Hospital of the Incurabili designed in 1590 by Francesco da Volterra. Both Peruzzi and Serlio had designed, but never built, oval-plan churches, whereas Volterra was able to reconcile the horizontal axis of a longitudinal plan with the vertical axis of a centralized and domical church to create a functional and intimate space for the lay congregation situated directly before the altar chapel that opens off the long end of the oval. After Volterra's death, his oval

161
162

160. Colossal Corinthian columns line the nave of San Salvatore in Lauro in Rome (1591), conjuring up the grandeur of ancient Rome.

161, 162. Francesco da Volterra designed San Giacomo in Augusta in Rome (1590) on an oval plan which established a clear, directional interior culminating in the tall barrel-vaulted chapel that houses the high altar. The church was part of the hospital complex of the Incurabili.

church of San Silvestro in Capite, designed in 1595, and the façade of San Giacomo in Augusta were completed by Maderno, who had come to Rome in the mid-1570s. Maderno, who eventually managed to inherit Fontana's, Volterra's, and Della Porta's patrons, designed the Palazzo Serlupi-Crescenzi in 1585, and the Palazzo Mattei di Giove in 1598 for Asdrubale Mattei, whose collection of ancient reliefs and portrait busts were inset in the courtyard façade and loggias, indicating the continued fascination with and importance of the antique in late sixteenth-century Rome. This antique and Early Christian revival was brought to the fore in the period leading up to the jubilee in 1600, celebrated during the reign of Clement VIII Aldobrandini (1536–1605), elected in 1592. It was led by Cesare Baronio who restored his own church of Saints Nereo and Achilleo in 1596–97, and included Cardinal Benedetto Giustiniani who had Carlo Lambardi (1554–1620) restore the church of Santa Prisca on the Aventine hill in 1600. The impact of Filippo Neri, who had explored the catacombs together with Charles Borromeo in the 1560s and who founded the Oratorians in 1575 aiming to return to the simplicity of the Early Christian Church, was considerable. Neri sponsored Baronio's *Annales Ecclesiasticæ* published in 1588, and Neri, Baronio, Antonio Gallonio and other Oratorians also promoted the Early Christian revival at their church of San Girolamo della Carità. So too Montano, together with Girolamo Rainaldi (1570–1655), restored and rebuilt the church of the woodcarvers and carpenters, San Giuseppe dei Falegnami in 1597, establishing a direct link with the ancient remains in the adjacent forum, an approach that would be taken up by Cortona in 1634 when designing the church of Saints Luca and Martina.

A different architectural direction was initiated by Maderno in his façade of Santa Susanna, begun in 1597, which has boldly projecting columns and pilasters and a clear focus on the central aedicules of both storeys. After Della Porta's death Clement VIII (for whom Maderno and Giovanni Fontana completed the villa and water theatre at Frascati) appointed Maderno chief architect at St Peter's. For Paul V, elected in 1605, Maderno submitted designs for the completion of the church as did Ludovico Cigoli (1559–1613) and others. In 1607 Paul V decided to complete the church with a long nave and façade brought to completion by Maderno in 1612. The Lombard Flaminio Ponzio was appointed official papal architect by Paul V and made an important contribution to the design of the Palazzo Borghese; in 1605 he designed the Cappella Paolina in Santa Maria Maggiore to house the tombs of Paul V and his predecessor Clement VIII, employing lavish coloured marbles and rich stuccoes, in a decisive shift away from reformation austerity. Ponzio, who had become a founding member of Academy of Saint Luke in 1593, designed the Acqua Paola in 1610. His most interesting project for Paul V was the reconstruction in 1609 of San Sebastiano above the catacombs of the martyr. Ponzio designed a palace-façade style upper floor surmounted by a triangular pediment,

165

163
164

166

167

163, 164. After completing the nave, Maderno designed the façade of St Peter's (1612), but this was compromised in execution because the flanking bell-towers were not built owing to structural problems.

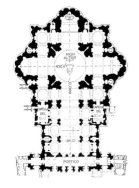

165. Carlo Maderno's façade
for Santa Susanna in Rome
(1597) heralds a new departure
with its dynamic composition.

166. The double-storey
arcade that divides the courtyard
of the Palazzo Borghese in Rome
from the secret garden beyond
is one of the most unusual
and innovative in Rome.

above an open arcaded ground floor. This project was completed by Giovanni Vansanzio (*c.* 1550–1621) who also worked with Ponzio on Scipione Borghese's villa on the Pincio from 1605 to 1613. The insertion of antique reliefs into the upper façade of the villa Borghese follows the extraordinary example set at the nearby villa transformed in 1566 by Baccio Bigio and Annibale de'Lippi, which was acquired in 1576 by Ferdinando I, Grand Duke of Tuscany, and subsequently known as the Villa Medici. There the pairs of beautiful matching reliefs across the eastern façade could only have been achieved by a ruthless spoliation and dismemberment of whole sarcophagi. By comparison, for his nearby palace on the Piazza Trinità dei Monti Federico Zuccari,

167. Flaminio Ponzio designed the Acqua Paola set on the Janiculum hill in Rome (1610–12) on the model of a triumphal arch.

as befitting his role as head of the Academy of Saint Luke, created a distinctly modern idiom that included bizarrerie and contrasted with his earlier employment of antique reliefs, inserted by Zuccari into the façade of his palace in Florence 1577–79.

Some Italian duchies and the Papal States

When the Medici were granted Granducal status in 1569 they consolidated their rule over all Tuscany, including feifdoms such as Pisa conquered in 1509. The city was protected by new fortifications, and humanist and scientific studies flourished there, including the founding of a botanical garden in 1543 by the doctor and botanist Luca Ghini, and the later scientific work of Galileo Galilei (1564–1612). Following his foundation of the Knights of Santo Stefano to combat Turkish pirates in 1561, Cosimo I asked Vasari in 1562 to redesign an existing square as the Piazza dei Cavalieri, comprising the Palazzo dell'Orologio 168 begun in 1564, and the church of Santo Stefano dei Cavalieri 169 begun in 1565 for which Cosimo I's illegitimate son Giovanni de' Medici (1566–1621), who was an architectural enthusiast, designed the elegant façade in 1593. Other practical buildings, such as the Medici arsenal were built in 1588, just as Francesco I and Ferdinando I instigated practical schemes for fortifying

168, 169. Vasari's urban intervention transformed the Piazza dei Cavalieri in Pisa (1562). The elegant façade of the church of Santo Stefano dei Cavalieri (1593), by Giovanni de'Medici, was executed in white, grey and pale pink marble and displayed the arms of the military order in the raised pediment.

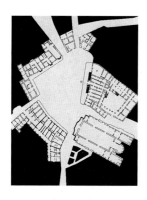

the harbour of Livorno, executed by Buontalenti from 1574. In Pisa Ferdinando I also commissioned Cosimo Pugliani (d.1618) to build the Logge dei Banchi on the river front which housed the wool and silk markets under its rectangular structure of tall arcades.

In Florence, Ferdinando I founded a 'workshop for hard stones' in 1588, the *Opificio di Pietre Dure*, that trained artisans to provide the material required to satisfy the developing taste for coloured marbles – parallel to that displayed by the popes in Rome at the Pauline and Sistine chapels of Santa Maria Maggiore, and evident in the architectural and sculptural ensemble of the high altar of Santo Spirito in Florence of 1599 by Giovanni Battista Caccini (1556–1613). Caccini had trained in Rome with Dosio and come with him to Florence in 1575 to work on the Gaddi chapel in Santa Maria Novella. The major project of the Opificio was the monumental task of building the Capella Medici (the Capella dei Principi) at San Lorenzo. An original project by Vasari was reworked by Buontalenti in numerous designs, but around 1600 Giovanni de' Medici made several designs which Ferdinand I preferred but had Buontalenti modify, resulting in one of the most extraordinary works of the period: a tall, cylindrical mausoleum, top-lit from an oculus and entirely

170

revetted in coloured stones. This display of magnificence was executed by Matteo Nigetti (1560–1648), a collaborator and assistant of Buontalenti's, who directed work there from 1608 until the completion of the chapel in 1643. A new phase in architecture was begun during the reign of Grand Duke Cosimo II de' Medici (1590–1621) from 1609, who had been taught architecture by Giulio Parigi (who had himself studied with his greatuncle Ammannati, and the Ducal architect Buontalenti, to whose post Parigi succeeded in 1608). Gherardo Silvano (1579–1675) renovated the Santissima Annunziata in 1612 at the start of a long and fruitful career, and Giulio Parigi, who was appointed head of the cathedral workshop, was best known for his scenographic and festival designs, executed with his eldest son Alfonso (1606–56), and for his design of the villa Poggio Imperiale built in 1622. The Parigi's engineering expertise played an important part in their work on the Isolotto of 1617 and the Amphitheatre of 1630 in the Boboli Gardens.

After 1505 the province of Bologna, immediately north of Tuscany, belonged to the Papal States. In the 1560s Pius IV instigated renovation work on the Piazza of Neptune adjacent to the central Piazza Maggiore on which Vignola imposed visual order with his scheme for the classical arcading of the Portico dei Banchi designed in 1561. The various proposals to complete the adjacent church of San Petronio, where Charles V was crowned Holy Roman Emperor by Clement VII in 1530, presented problems because the original design of 1518 for a Tuscan Gothic façade by Domenico Aimo (c. 1460–1539) was out of date when construction begun in the 1560s under the direction of Antonio Terribilia. Yet the solutions proposed to this frustrating project by Peruzzi, Vignola and others were little more convincing, just as those presented by Domenico Tibaldi (1541–c. 83), and the classicizing solutions of Palladio and Francesco Terribilia also remained on paper. Antonio Terribilia did, however, successfully design and execute the adjacent Palazzo dell'Archiginnasio in 1561–63, one of the first purpose-built university complexes comprising a long sequence of classrooms located over the arcaded loggia of the façade. There was also a specially designed anatomy theatre built in 1638, modelled on that of Padua University built in 1594. One of the most imposing and innovative buildings in Bologna was San Salvatore, designed in 1613 by the Barnabite monk Giovanni Ambrogio Magenta (1565–1635) of Milan, who became General of the Order in 1612. Magenta, who became a friend of Cassiano del Pozzo, was an engineer,

171. Giovanni Ambrogio Magenta designed the austere but monumental Barnabite church of San Salvatore in Bologna (1613–20) in white stone and plaster; giant fluted Corinthian columns and pilasters line the nave.

171

mathematician, and theoretician, who helped renovate the cathedral of Bologna, San Pietro, following Domenico Tibaldi's construction of the choir in 1575; he also designed the Barnabite church of San Paolo in 1611, for which Bernini would execute the high altar, and Alessandro Algardi (1598–1654) its sculptural ensemble, in the 1630s.

Unlike Bologna, in the sixteenth century Ferrara was an independent duchy ruled by members of the Este family including Alfonso I (1476–34) who reigned from 1505, Ercole II who reigned from 1534, and Alfonso II who reigned from 1559 and under whose rule Ferrara became one of the most splendid courts in Northern Italy. In 1567 Ligorio became curator of Alfonso II's collection of antiquities, and in 1575 Giovan Battista Aleotti was appointed ducal architect and military engineer and worked with Marcantonio Pasi (1537–99) on the city's fortifications. But in 1598, Ferrara was placed under direct papal rule because the reign of Cesare of the Montecchio Este was considered invalid, and he was forced to retreat to Modena, where he set up a new capital. Aleotti remained in Ferrara as architect to the city: he built a pentagonal fortress in 1608, the theatres of San Lorenzo in 1606 and the Sala Grande in 1612, and together with Alessandro Balbi remodelled the Palazzo Paradiso as the seat of the university between 1586–1610. Aleotti also designed the oval-plan church of San Carlo designed in 1612 with a robustly sculptural façade with projecting semi-columns, and for Enzo Bentivoglio (1575–1639) the theatre of the Accademia degli Intrepidi in 1605–06, of which Bentivoglio was principe. For Cesare d'Este in 1600 Aleotti designed the fortifications of the town of Scandiano, and fitted out the impressive fortified 172 villa there with a curved double-ramp staircase set within a small rotunda surmounted with an elegant eight-ribbed dome rising to an oculus, a form later taken up in the work of Gaspare Vigarini (1588–1663) for the rotunda of San Girolamo and Vitale in Reggio Emilia of 1646. The most notable of many projects d'Este initiated in Modena was the Ducal Palace begun in 1630, for which opinions were subsequently sought from a number of architects including Girolamo Rainaldi, Bartolomeo Avanzini (1600–58), Bernini, Borromini, and Cortona. In Reggio Emilia, the second city of the Estense duchy, the most important work of the period was the Santuario della Ghiara, designed in 1596 by Alessandro Balbi, whose Greek-cross plan was chosen in preference to Aleotti's in competition.

On either side of the Po, between Reggio Emilia and Mantua,

172. Giambattista Aleotti created a curved double branch staircase at the Rocca di Scandiano (1600) that ingeniously exploited the small circular space that Aleotti transformed into a grand architectural composition replete with paired columns on pedestals framing arches containing figure sculpture set within aedicules.

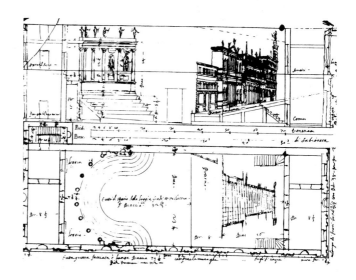

lay the cities of Guastalla and Sabbioneta which formed part of
the Gonzaga duchy, and which were both developed in the 1550s
by minor members of the family led by dukes Federico II from
1519, Francesco III (1533–50) from 1540, Guglielmo (1538–87)
from 1550, and Vincenzo I (1562–1612) from 1587. At
Guastalla, Cesare Gonzaga (1533–75) had Domenico Giunti
construct a pentagonal fortified city wall, and the cathedral was
designed in the 1570s by Francesco da Volterra. Sabbioneta in
Lombardy was planned from 1554 as an ideal Ducal city complex by the architectural enthusiast Vespasiano Gonzaga, who
was inspired by the writings of Vitruvius and Alberti. The fortified city included the Palazzo del Giardino, built in 1584 on a
very long and narrow site, which was connected by an elevated
passageway to the adjacent Gallery of Antiquities, a one-hun-
dred-metre-long antiquarium above a continuous ground-floor
portico, that housed the Duke's collection – one of the first purpose–built structures of its kind. Other buildings included an
imposing city gate, a church and hospital, as well as a theatre the 173
Duke commissioned from Scamozzi in 1588. Scamozzi designed 174
the first autonomous theatre of the early modern period,
creating a public building by locating it at one end of a large
block of contiguous buildings, and distinguishing it with three
elaborately articulated façades complete with Latin inscriptions
on the string course between the two storeys proclaiming
Gonzaga's aim at recreating the splendours of ancient Rome.

Scamozzi's design presented a decisive shift away from temporary theatres and those built within palaces, and his project sketch depicts the theatre in longitudinal section and plan, revealing innovations such as the stage with its receding perspectival sets, the proscenium, and the horse-shoe shaped *cavea* or auditorium, enclosed with a screen of columns supporting figure sculpture, from behind which the duke could view performances.

Scamozzi's theatre directly influenced that designed by Aleotti for the Farnese Dukes of Parma, one of the greatest Italian courts of the late sixteenth century. In 1545, the year Paul III summoned the Council in Trent, he also created the Duchy of Castro comprising Parma and Piacenza, for his son Pier Luigi, thus bringing this area under the control of the church. Pier Luigi's ambitious plans for the capital in Piacenza were never carried out as he was murdered there in 1547. Although his brother Ottavio, who ruled 1547–86 (with a brief interruption in 1549–50), transferred the capital to Parma, in 1558 Ottavio commissioned the Palazzo in Piacenza from Francesco Paciotto Vignola, who was in Parma intermittently in the 1560s working on the Palazzo del Giardino, also assumed control of the building in Piacenza in 1564. Although he left it unfinished, he designed a theatre for the courtyard as well as designing the gardens there for Ottavio and Cardinal Ranuccio in the 1570s, at the same time as he and Del Duca were laying out the Orti Farnesiani on the Palatine hill in Rome for Cardinal Alessandro Farnese. In Parma, several parts of Palazzo della Pilotta were executed for Ranuccio I (1569–1622) by Simone Moschino (1553–1610) from Orvieto who designed the grandiose staircase in 1604 comprising a single wide flight that arrived at a landing situated under a domed octagonal volume. This was succeeded by twin return flights that originally led to the palace armoury, which was converted by Aleotti into a temporary theatre in 1618. Aleotti designed tiered seating on a U-shaped plan with a double-storey arcade based on Palladio's Basilica as the backdrop for the audience. This motif influenced the design of many subsequent theatre galleries in subsequent theatres. The proscenium differed from those at the Teatro Olimpico and Sabbioneta, and was the first to use stage wings built of wooden frames on wheeled undercarriages that allowed scenery to be more rapidly changed.

Giovanni Battista Fornovo (1530–85) was a military architect who had worked for the Farnese at Caprarola and at

175. Aleotti's Theatre (1618), built in the Palazzo della Pilotta in Parma, included a deep horseshoe shaped seating area that could accommodate a large audience (destroyed 1944 and later reconstructed).

Piacenza. In 1560 he designed San Quintino in Parma, and for Ottavio Farnese he built the Santissima Annunziata of the Frati Minori in 1566. The oval central space is surrounded by radiating chapels with large windows that create a luminous interior, while the exterior cleverly combines convex and concave curves that adumbrate seventeenth-century developments in Rome, and ideas that would be taken up by the Modenese Guarino Guarini (1624–83) in the church of the Consolata at Turin, and by Filippo Juvarra (1678–1736), who drew the plan of the church in his travel diary of 1716. A second innovative church, the hexagonal plan Santa Maria del Quartiere, was designed in 1604 by Giovan Battista Magnani (1571–1653) – perhaps with the help of Aleotti – in the military quarter of the city, dominated by the Citadella of Parma designed in 1591 by Genesio Bresciani (1525–1610) and Giovanni Antonio Stirpio (d. 1592). Magnani, who designed the Fountain Cloister at San Paolo in 1613, was subsequently appointed city architect in 1622. In the second half of the sixteenth century Parma overtook Bologna as the greatest city in Emilia, but Bologna remained the central crossroad for those travelling north from Florence, and those travelling along the via Emilia from the Marches at Rimini to Bologna, Modena, Reggio, Parma and Piacenza, before heading into Lombardy and its capital Milan.

176–178

North-western Italy

The three major cities of north-western Italy were all affected by their relation to the Habsburgs. Although nominally independent, Genoa continued to thrive on its close links with Spain. Gian Andrea I Doria (1540–1606) and his wife encouraged church-building by the New Orders such as the Carmelites' Sant' Anna of 1584, and the Gesù designed by Valeriano in 1589. Andrea Vannone (d. 1619) designed both Santa Maria Maddalena in 1585 for the Somascans, and San Siro for the Theatines in 1586. Gio. Francesco Balbi commissioned Bartolomeo Bianco (*c.* 1590–*c.* 1657) to design a new street named after his family in 1616, based on the model of the Strada Nuova, and Bianco also designed the innovative Jesuit College in the 1630s. The Spanish domination of Milan was recognized in 1559 with the treaty of Cateau-Cambrésis, and the same treaty liberated Piedmont from French rule and returned it to the House of Savoy. The tenth Duke, Emanuele Filiberto, had Paciotto of Urbino undertake fortifications in 1564 including a pentagonal citadel for the new capital Turin, and his successor

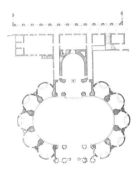

176, 177, 178. Giovanni Battista Fornovo designed the Santissima Annunziata in Parma (1566) on a transverse oval plan with surrounding apsidal chapels that contrast with the concave upper bays of the exterior and the tall projecting portico, all executed in fine brickwork. The vault was rebuilt by Girolamo Rainaldi (1626).

179. This drawing signed by 'Monsa' of the Piazza Castello in Turin records the renovations effected by Ascanio Vitozzi to create a square surrounded by porticoes.

from 1580 Carlo Emanuele I (1562–1630) appointed Ascanio Vitozzi (1539–1615) ducal architect and engineer in 1584, and commissioned him to complete the modernization of Turin.

The heart of the city was reorganized with new streets which cut through the crowded medieval centre such as the Contrada Nuova, and the Contrada dei Panierai that connected the Piazza Castello at San Lorenzo to the Palazzo di Città. Vitozzi began reconstruction of the Palazzo Ducale in 1584 and created a new principal façade that faced south onto Piazza Castello which served as its forecourt. The piazza itself was regularized with the provision of ground floor porticoes which served as the base structure for the subsequent palaces which lined it. Porticoes were also used for the newly constructed Contrada Nuova, designed in 1587, that connected Piazza Castello to Piazza San Carlo, and led southwards out to the extraurban Ducal residence at Mirafiore. In 1612, the section of road immediately beyond the city walls was extended and developed to form the blueprint for the development in the 1620s of the Città Nuova to the south.

For Carlo Emanuele I, Vitozzi, together with Giacomo Soldati, built the centralized church of Santa Maria dei Cappuccini in 1585. It was located half-way up the Monte dei Cappuccini, on the other side of the Po, where it functioned as a Sacro Monte, similar to the 1565 project by Alessi at Varallo. The Duke also commissioned a new sanctuary to house the miracle-working Madonna of the large and populous town of Mondovì, located between Turin and Genoa, which he had subjugated as part of the consolidation of his rule. Numerous designs for Santa Maria di Vicoforte were submitted by the Governor of Savigliano, Count Ercole Negro di Sanfront (1541–1622), but the project eventually went to Vitozzi whose design of 1596, which envisaged the largest central-plan dome of the sixteenth century, built on his experience with the Cappuccins in Turin. Located on a hill outside Vicoforte, Vitozzi designed this freestanding pilgrimage church on an oval plan, contained within the rectangle established by the four corner towers (somewhat like Alessi's church in Genoa). He placed the miraculous image at the centre of the oval space, where it could immediately be seen by visitors entering the church via any of the three prominent façades, although Vitozzi maintained axiality within the church through the provision of a large entrance vestibule located at the end of the oval in its own space opposite the high altar. Vitozzi's work in Turin and Mondovì, together with his fortifications at Cherasco, provide a good example of the

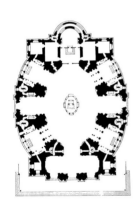

180. The long ends of the oval plan of Ascanio Vitozzi's Santa Maria at Mondovì (1596) contain the entrance and high altar; four chapels flank the transepts which contain entrances to enable processional movement around the miraculous image set in the middle of the church under the drum and dome that were built later by Francesco Gallo (1728–33).

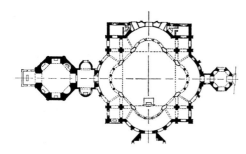

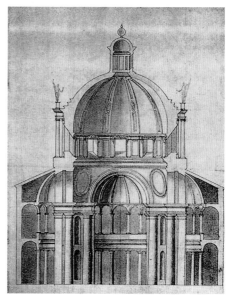

mobility of architects practising in the cities of northern Italy. Alessi worked in Genoa and Milan, but was also in Turin in 1569; Soldati worked briefly in Milan with Tibaldi in the 1570s, but otherwise practised in Turin where he was officially appointed engineer and architect in 1601, having successfully completed with Vitozzi a scheme to improve the road and waterworks there in 1597.

Two important architectural projects in late sixteenth-century Milan involved existing buildings: the ongoing construction of Milan's Gothic cathedral gave rise to a serious debate about the style it should be continued in; and the rebuilding of the dome of the fourth-century church of San Lorenzo, which had collapsed in 1573, presented problems of style, statics, and structure. Because the quatrefoil plan of the Early Christian church had to be maintained, Bassi created a structure of eight piers (paired under the short lengths of the unequal octagonal entablature) that enabled the enormous dome of over twenty metres diameter to spring from stable supports. Bassi's original design for the dome was modified in 1590, after criticism by the Roman architect Tolomeo Rinaldi (c. 1561–1637), so that the ribs of the drumless octagonal cupola rise directly from the entablature to the oculus, and the large windows also lighten the structure, which is supported externally by an octagonal drum surmounted by a shallow dome and lantern.

181
182

Bassi's classicizing vocabulary for the entablature and dome was only partially successful as the effect was somewhat top-heavy and ponderous when compared to the more refined fourth-century architecture below it.

Tibaldi's designs to transform the interior of Milan Cathedral with his litrugical furnishings were bitterly opposed by Bassi, who considered them inadequate. These objections were dismissed in the face of Borromeo's powerful support and the project went ahead, providing the cathedral with the necessary architectural solutions for the celebration of the liturgy. The problem of the façade remained. Both Tibaldi and Bassi (when he finally succeeded as head architect there in 1585 after Tibaldi resigned at Borromeo's death) produced numerous classicizing designs, but none of these were executed as they could not mask the fundamental problem of reconciling in a classical composition the tall vertical central nave section of the cathedral with the significantly lower flanking aisles. In their projects, both Tibaldi and Bassi resorted to the placement of obelisks on the lateral flanks of the façade, above the ground-floor order, to counterbalance the central second-storey order. The problem of placing a classicizing façade on a Gothic church, for which Alberti had presented an early solution at Santa Maria Novella in Florence in 1450, still exercised architects' imaginations over a hundred years later.

Other work by Bassi included the execution, in a reduced and simplified form, of Alessi's façade design for Santa Maria presso San Celso in 1570, and the completion of Alessi's San Vittore al Corpo in the 1580s. Bassi completed the choir and tribunes of Tibaldi's San Fedele, and in 1573 transformed Santa Maria della Passione from a Greek-cross plan into a Latin-cross plan through the addition of a long nave. With the support of Borromeo, Tibaldi designed the centralized plague church of San Sebastiano in 1577, the Jesuits' San Gaudenzio at Novara in Piedmont in 1576, and the important sanctuaries at Caravaggio 1571, Saronno 1578, and Rho 1583–84. Tibaldi left for Spain after Borromeo's death in 1584, but the work of church reform was taken up by Borromeo's cousin Federico, who had studied in Rome and at the Collegio Borromeo in Pavia, and who became a Cardinal in 1587, and Archbishop of Milan in 1595. In residence from 1601, Federico Borromeo renewed his uncle's pastoral visits, and founded the Ambrosiana as an official diocesan institution which published the *Museaum* in 1625. The Ambrosiana complex consisted of an Art Museum built in 1618, the Art

183. Giuseppe Maria Ricchino designed a curved façade for the Collegio Elvetico in Milan (1627). The window frames have no orders but employ prominent Michelangelesque pediments.

184, 185. Lorenzo Binago employed a Greek-cross plan for Sant'Alessandro in Milan (1601) with a large cupola over the central crossing, and five smaller, subsidiary domes. Every surface of the interior is lavishly decorated.

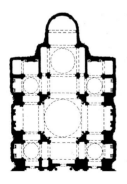

Academy established in 1620, and most notably the Library built 1603–30 by various architects including Buzzi, Fabio Mangone (1587–1629), and Francesco Maria Ricchino (1584–1658). Mangone, who was appointed the first architecture master of the Ambrosian Academy of Design in 1620, planned the Library with Buzzi on a longitudinal axis because of the deep but narrow site. The sequence of spaces also included an atrium, the main reading room, and a small open courtyard with porticoes, beyond which lay a meeting room and a manuscript room, while a stair led from the courtyard to the basement containing prohibited books. The reading room was much smaller than either Michelangelo's Medici library or that at the Vatican, and much closer to Juan de Herrera's library at the Escorial which was built for Philip II in 1584. It abandoned the idea of desks and chairs under windows and instead introduced very tall book cases lining the walls. The thermal widows at either end controlled the amount of natural light entering the reading room and harmonized perfectly with the barrel-vaulted ceiling.

There was a spate of church-building around the turn of the century in Milan, including the renovation of Santo Stefano by Giuseppe Meda (d. 1599) in 1596, San Babila from 1598 and San Sepolcro in 1605 by Aurelio Trezzi (d. 1625), and San Sisto from

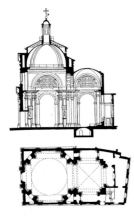

1600. Fabio Mangone led the cathedral workshop from 1617–29, after having trained there with his father Giambattista (1547–1627); he also designed the main building and courtyard of the Collegio Elvetico in 1608. The Barnabite monk Lorenzo Binago (1554–1629), who built San Paolo at Casale Monferrato in 1586 and the Barnabite church and college of the Santissima Annunziata at Zagarolo near Rome in 1593, arrived in Milan in 1599. Binago's first undertaking was the church of Sant' Alessandro, for which he produced a series of proposals in 1601, including octagonal, circular, and Greek-cross centralizing plans. Magenta also presented various schemes, and the Greek-cross plan with an extended choir that was eventually built was the product of collaboration between Binago and his pupil Ricchino. The extended chancel and choir of Sant'Alessandro established an axial interior direction within the centralized plan, and the mysterious, almost theatrical lighting emanating from the different sized domes, created a dramatic, rather than uniform interior as was the norm. Binago's design influenced that of later Barnabite churches such as San Carlo ai Catinari in Rome of 1612 by Rosato Rosati (1559–1622) and the new cathedral of Brescia designed in 1604 by Giovanni Battista Lantana (1581–1627).

183
184
185

Ricchino, who studied with Binago and subsequently in Rome, returned to Milan in 1603 and designed a series of innovative churches – many of them destroyed – and sketched projects for numerous others which demonstrate his fertile architectural imagination, including San Giovanni Battista in 1609, Santa Maria di Loreto in 1616, San Bartolomeo in 1623, and San Pietro con la Rete 1623. His most important surviving work is San Giuseppe, begun in 1607, which combines major and minor interpenetrating Greek-cross spaces for the congregation and the sanctuary, surmounted with major and minor cupolas in the north Italian fashion. On the exterior, each side of the octagonal upper drum is articulated differently, according to an ascending heirarchy from the large, low lateral windows, to the higher pedimented blind niches on the diagonal flanks, to the principal façade with its lavish semi-columns, balustraded window, and elaborate double pediment. Ricchino's attempt to integrate the upper level of the principal façade with the drum was only partially successful, and he resorted to freestanding Albertian volutes to connect the lower and upper sections of the façade.

186
187

For the Brera College Ricchino executed from 1625 the vast central courtyard and surrounding rooms designed to house the

186, 187. Ricchino's design for San Giuseppe in Milan (1607) consists of a domed octagonal lay space succeeded by a smaller domed rectangular chancel. On the short diagonal walls of the octagon, the giant Corinthian columns frame a doorway surmounted by a niche with sculpture and a small balconied aedicule, recalling the way Michelangelo squeezed architectural elements together in the New Sacristy at San Lorenzo in Florence.

Jesuit's school, library and observatory. In 1627 he designed an innovative concave façade with a central convex balcony for the Collegio Elvetico, a design that foreshadows subsequent developments in seventeenth-century architecture, including Borromini's Oratory of the Filippini begun in 1637. Ricchino

was eventually appointed chief architect of the cathedral in 1630 and made several designs for the façade, but it was his numerous Milanese churches and the drawings for them that were most influential on the following generation. Indeed, Milan between the 1570s and the 1620s produced more intellectual and sophisticated architectural design than anywhere else in Italy. It was also the city through which all the Ticinese architects such as Maderno passed on their way to Rome. Milan was the only place where a young architect often received a proper training in both Gothic and classic design, as well as a technical and structural training equal to that available in the workshop of St Peter's. It is no surprise that Borromini trained in the cathedral workshop at Milan before transferring to Rome where he also trained in the workshop at St Peter's under Carlo Maderno. The importance of Milan cannot be underestimated as the conduit for architects moving south to Rome; but the impact of Milanese architecture also spread to other centres in northern Italy.

Longhena, Cortona, Bernini and Borromini: the creation of the Baroque

The innovative architectural achievements of Ricchino and others were taken up and developed most significantly by Borromini, who trained in Milan. Longhena was influenced by Lombard architecture, but by comparison, both Cortona from Tuscany and the nominally Neapolitan Bernini were the products of training in Rome. The decade from around 1624 was exciting architecturally because it was then that Longhena, Cortona, Bernini, and Borromini, having been born in the years 1597–99, came to maturity. All four also received their first significant and independent architectural commissions around this time: Bernini's Santa Bibiana in 1624, Longhena's Santa Maria della Salute in 1631, Cortona's Santi Luca and Martina and Borromini's San Carlo alle Quattro Fontane both in 1634. Innovation clearly outweighs tradition in the design of these four outstanding works, and they are usually considered as heralding the creation of Baroque architecture.

Longhena's pioneering design for Santa Maria della Salute 188–190 of 1631 had an immediate impact locally, but his ideas only became influential beyond Venice much later in the century. Selected as the winning entry in competition, Longhena's project comprised a sequence of interrelated but relatively autonomous spaces including a domed rotonda surrounded by an ambulatory, a domed apsidal sanctuary, and a choir for the

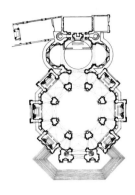

188, 189, 190. Baldassare Longhena's unusual plan for Santa Maria della Salute in Venice (1631) combined an octagonal rotunda with an apsidal sanctuary and rectangular monks' choir. The unusual exterior has two differently sized domes and figure sculpture set on top of the large scrolls that surround the drum.

conventuals beyond the high altar, which together fulfilled the complex requirements of the Venetian Senate who commissioned the building, including the need to accommodate participants in the annual ceremony of thanksgiving for deliverance from the plague. The centralized building had a prominent longitudinal axis that established a series of privileged viewpoints including that from the principal entrance to high altar, and the extraordinary vistas which open up from the centre of the rotunda into each of the chapels opening off the ambulatory. The scenographic effects of the interior are matched by the spectacular exterior profile that Longhena created through the compositional strategy of situating adjacent to one another the two domes of unequal size – one small and plain, and flanked by two bell-towers; the other enormous and surrounded by striking volutes and figure sculpture at drum level. Prominently sited, this monumental building functioned as a landmark that radically altered the urban landscape of Venice.

That Longhena at the age of 34 was able to envisage such an extraordinary, indeed audacious project, reveals an ambitious architect. His training in stonemasonry with his father enabled him to provide a sound structure for his unusual design, while his intellectual training, received when he was tutored by Scamozzi in the years 1614–16, enabled him to devise the functionally and iconographically sophisticated design. Longhena transformed traditional Venetian architectural vocabulary through striking compositional effects and moved beyond the traditional medium of pen and ink for presentation drawings to employ pencil in design sketches for the alterations to his original plan, an innovation in method that Borromini perfected as an art. When commissioning Santa Maria della Salute, the Venetian Senate wrote to Rome to enquire if the Cavaliere Bernini could be persuaded to sculpt a statue of the Virgin for the high altar of the church. The disconcerting reply from the Venetian Ambassador at Rome was that he feared the sculpture either would be delivered very late or it would not be by Bernini, who was busy, together with Cortona and Borromini, creating the fundamental works of the Roman Baroque.

The Rome in which Borromini arrived in 1619, after training for ten years at Milan Cathedral under Andrea Biffi (c. 1581–c. 1630), was dominated by long established workshops such as that of Onorio Longhi (1568–1619) and his son Martino the Younger (1602–60), who were then engaged on the construction of Santi Ambrogio e Carlo al Corso. The largest and most impor-

tant workshop was that of St Peter's run by Maderno, which
Borromini joined because a relative of his, Leone Garvo, worked
there until falling to his death from a scaffold in 1620. As the
most important architect then in Rome, Maderno often acted in
a supervisory capacity for other projects, such as the building of
Sant'Ignazio from 1624–27, following the canonization in 1622
of Ignatius and Francis Xavier (1506–52) by Gregory XV
Ludovisi (1554–1623) elected 1521. There Maderno, together
with Paolo Maruscelli (1596–1649), supervised and modified
the designs of Orazio Grassi (1583–1654), based on those of
Domenichino (1581–1641), but it was Grassi who then supervised the construction of the church. Maderno was also responsible in the 1620s for the construction of the Theatines' Sant'
Andrea della Valle, and he encouraged his talented young pro-
tégé to produce detailed designs for the façade around 1621.

In the same years Bernini was undertaking his first significant architectural commission for Maffeo Barberini, who was
elected Urban VIII in 1623 and who, for the impending jubilee
year of 1625, embarked on the restoration of Santa Bibiana,
which lay on the pilgrimage route between the basilicas of Santa
Maria Maggiore and San Lorenzo fuori le mura. In 1624 Bernini
sensitively adapted the interior of the small medieval church
through the addition of a chancel to house the high altar, for

191. Gianlorenzo Bernini
renovated the church of
Santa Bibiana in Rome (1624)
and added the small chancel to
house his sculpture of the saint.

191

192. Gianlorenzo Bernini was appointed by Urban VIII to design a Baldacchino for St Peter's (1624). Made of bronze, gilded and almost 29 metres high, it is an architectural sculpture composed of four twisted columns supporting a canopy (completed 1633).

which he also sculpted the figure of Bibiana. Bernini was already famous as a sculptor of striking individual works, but here the finely carved sculpture was specifically created for a particular setting. It was illuminated by carefully directed lighting effects, achieved architecturally through the placement of windows within the vault – a device Bernini would subsequently develop for his famous sculptural ensemble of Saint Teresa in Ecstasy. Bernini also added a two-storey palace-type church façade with ground floor arcades, based on that created by Ponzio in his renovation of the church of San Sebastiano fuori le mura in 1611; this type was subsequently used by Soria when renovating San Gregorio Magno from 1629. Pietro da Cortona was also employed at Santa Bibiana, producing his first major fresco cycle depicting episodes from the life of the saint. But in these years Urban VIII's preference was always for Bernini, whom he had asked in 1624 to design a new baldacchino for the high altar of St Peter's, thereby bringing together in the same workshop Bernini and Borromini.

This crucial commission for an architectural sculpture, or sculptural architecture, demonstrates the genius of both Bernini

193, 194. Francesco Borromini supplied most of the detailed drawings (1631) of individual elements such as the twisted column and Composite capital of the Baldacchino, and represented the very fine detailed sculptural work, including the delicate foliage, that would be rendered in the bronze casting. Borromini also produced the concept drawing that calculated the relationship of the Baldacchino structure to the interior space of St Peter's, including the four main piers of the crossing, one of which is seen to the left, and the height of the entablature above the pier and the coffered vaulting of the apse behind the crossing

195, 196. Gianlorenzo Bernini's sketches (1631) for the Baldacchino document his experimentation with the various decorative details of the canopy.

and Borromini and the enormous differences between their creative processes. Although Bernini was in charge of the project, based on Maderno's concept of four twisted bronze columns supporting a canopy, the earliest surviving drawings for the structure are by Borromini, who carefully rendered the various details of the baldacchino including the lintel in the form of a tasselled drapery, the impost block and entablature, and the upper portion of a column and its Composite 193 capital. Borromini's finely detailed presentation drawings in pen and ink communicate the precise form of the structure to be cast. By contrast, the drawings in graphite for the same project reveal his effort to determine suitable overall proportions 194 for the baldacchino in relation to the vast interior of St Peter's. Bernini's subsequent ink sketches for the canopy, which record his concept of the project, were executed in just a few strokes 195 and indicate his completely different approach to design. 196 Further sketches in chalk record Bernini's numerous variations for the decorative details of the canopy, some of which were then worked up in ink.

Urban VIII's next major undertaking involved the contributions of all the Barberini family's artistic protégés. Francesco 197

Barberini acquired a site adjacent to the Quattro Fontane in 1625, on which to build a palace. Although Cortona submitted a grandiose project, it would have been too expensive to build and instead Maderno was entrusted to design a residence (now known as the Palazzo Barberini) that was part palace and part suburban villa, comprising a principal block divided on the piano nobile by a central *salone* shared by Taddeo Barberini and Cardinal Francesco, whose flanking apartments extended into the two lateral wings. After Maderno's death in 1629, Bernini directed the project with the assistance of Borromini, who again provided detailed designs for important aspects of the building, such as the circular staircase and the perspectival windows on the upper floor. At the same time Bernini was also put in charge of building at St Peter's; Borromini worked in a subordinate position at both sites for three years 1629–32 before falling out with Bernini, who was paid ten times more than Borromini and received all the credit for these works. Cortona, who designed the riding court at Palazzo Barberini, avoided directly competing with Bernini in this instance by turning to painting, and executing his most important fresco decorations in the *salone* and adjacent rooms of the palace.

195
196
197

197. Carlo Maderno, Gianlorenzo Bernini and Francesco Borromini all contributed to the design of the Palazzo Barberini in Rome (1625–33). The 'perspective' windows of the upper floor were designed by Borromini, as were the unusual window frames of the flanking bays.

Cortona's first work as an independent architect came as a result of his election as head of the Academy of Saint Luke in 1634 when he decided to personally pay for the renovation of the crypt of their church of Saint Martina adjacent to the Roman Forum. Upon the discovery of Martina's relics Francesco Barberini decided to help fund the rebuilding of the entire church and Cortona designed an innovative Greek-cross plan with a tall, illusionistic, ribbed and coffered dome over the crossing, and an interior wall articulation composed of giant columns and piers. The gently protruding convex façade, bulging out from between the lateral pilasters that seem to restrain it, is one of three extraordinary curved façades designed around this time, including Borromini's façade for the Oratory of the Filippini designed 1637 and his façade designs for San Carlo alle Quattro Fontane of 1634–38.

198. Borromini's drawing (1634, 1638 and later) records the ground plan of the projected complex at San Carlo alle Quattro Fontane in Rome, including the residential wing (built 1634–35), the cloister (built 1635–36), and the church (begun 1638).

199. The cloister of Borromini's San Carlo alle Quattro Fontane in Rome (1635–36) has Tuscan columns set-off from the corners, and unusual curved lintels between the paired columns.

200, 201. (Overleaf) The fluid interior space of Borromini's San Carlo alle Quattro Fontane in Rome (begun 1638) is combined with an illusionistic cupola.

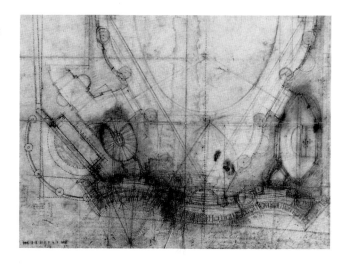

202. This drawing records Borromini's substantial reworking of the façade design for San Carlo alle Quattro Fontane in Rome at the time of its construction (begun 1665).

For San Carlo, Borromini in 1634 initially designed, within the restricted site limited by the via Felice and the via Pia (and the existing and immovable fountain where these two streets met) a dormitory, refectory, cloister, and small church for the Spanish Discalced Trinitarians. Before beginning construction in 1636, Borromini revised the design of the rectangular cloister and replaced the corner piers with Tuscan columns set-off from the corners, establishing an elongated octagon at roof level, and convex corner segments at ground and balustrade level, where the unusual design of the triangular balusters with alternating upper and lower bulbs provides greater transparency, and also indicates Borromini's propensity to rethink and redesign each individual element of the architectural vocabulary employed in this building. In 1638 Borromini enlarged the plan of the church and extended the arms of the abbreviated Greek-cross all the way to the via Felice; but the loss of the sacristy was unacceptable to the monks and Borromini redesigned the church once more, reinstating the sacristy and creating instead fictive Greek-cross arms, represented by the lateral niches with perspectival coffering. These niches form part of the undulating membrane of columns set into, but also projecting from the perimeter wall that encloses this fluid, almost elastic, interior space. The columns delimit each concave niche but can also be read as continuing in convex sets of four from one niche to the next, establishing a continuous articulation of the interior space. The key to Borromini's composition can be found by reading the entablature that delineates a diamond shape (composed of two equilat-

198

199

200

eral triangles), of which only four straight elements remain, because the other sections have been replaced with the four concave bays. Above the entablature four arches and pendentives establish a transitional zone that separates the lower practical space of worship from the heavenly zone above, demarcated by the substantial elliptical ring above which the drumless cupola rises. The cupola is top-lit through the lantern and by four windows located directly above the ring which are the same size and shape as the octagonal coffers that (along with the lozenge and cross-shaped coffers) create the illusionistically extended cupola.

The interior of San Carlo was complete by the 1640s and it won instant fame and notoriety for its architect. It was the first building since those of Michelangelo and Palladio in which every single detail was minutely designed and which established a significantly new interpretation of architectural space and vocabulary. This little church demonstrates and encapsulates, more than any other building of the period, the radical innovations in design that immediately altered architectural developments in Rome and then spread throughout Italy and eventually Europe.

Epilogue: Like Michelangelo's Medici Library begun just over a century earlier, Borromini's San Carlo alle Quattro Fontane heralded a new departure in architecture – referred to as the baroque. Yet Borromini's design process, documented in his numerous drawings, reveals exactly the opposite qualities to those usually associated with the baroque, such as a tendency to exaggeration, bombast and rhetoric. Instead, at San Carlo and in all his subsequent commissions, Borromini approached the task of design, which usually involved a difficult or limited site, with great deliberateness, care, and attention to detail. He repeatedly rethought and redesigned the plan, elevation, and each individual element, using his profound knowledge of geometry and mathematics to create innovative spatial forms. Borromini indeed heralded a new and modern way of designing architectural space and vocabulary, breaking out of the norms of the past, to create a deliberately ambiguous interior for San Carlo. It is no surprise then that it was Michelangelo, above all other architects, that Borromini esteemed and was influenced by – indeed one could say that the adumbration of baroque spatial forms in Michelangelo's late Sforza chapel, which had lain dormant since the 1560s, were finally understood, explored and developed by Borromini, whose works usher in a distinctly new era in architectural design as significant as that inaugurated by Michelangelo's Medici Library.

Borromini reused and elaborated throughout his career the particular approach to design with which he had achieved such spectacular results at San Carlo. For example, in his next commission of 1637, obtained by ousting Paolo Maruscelli as architect with the help of his lifelong supporter Virgilio Spada (1596–1662), Borromini designed a curved façade for the Oratory and House of the Filippini. This was built in brick, in order not to compete with the adjacent church of Santa Maria in Vallicella, yet Borromini managed to conjure up the grandeur of the ancient Roman buildings he had studied so intensely, as well as creating a sophisticated palace-like complex of interiors, including a grandiose staircase and large rooms with imposing, sculptural fireplaces. Borromini's original project comprised a five-bay façade in fine brickwork with two flanking bays of rougher brickwork, and a narrower upper storey. But when the Oratorians decided, in August 1638, to change the location of their library and situate it behind the upper storey of the oratory façade, Borromini altered his design and, in order to maintain the proportional relation between the new width and height of

156

the upper façade, he visually incorporated the flanking bays into façade proper, now seven bays wide. The same strategy was later used by Borromini for the façade of the Collegio di Propoganda Fide near the Piazza di Spagna, which again only partially corresponds to the internal spatial configuration. This was the art of visual deception, *lo inganno degl'occhi*, that Borromini, following the exempla of Michelangelo and Palladio, employed to such great effect, making something look visually right even if it was irregular or did not correspond with the rest of the building.

The interior of the Oratory of the Filippini, finished by 1639, has only two spatial zones (unlike San Carlo which has three), consisting of a lower zone for worshippers and an upper zone with windows and an area for singers at one end. A similar two-zone schema was employed for Sant'Ivo alle Sapienza of 1642

203. Borromini's drum and spire of Sant'Ivo (1640s–50s) is set above Giacomo della Porta's courtyard (1560s) of the University of Rome, called the Sapienza, establishing a remarkable contrast between the concave termination of the courtyard and the convex drum above.

and the chapel of the Re Magi at the Collegio di Propaganda Fide of 1660. Both these spaces have a tall lower zone articulated by giant pilasters and windows situated immediately above the entablature; in the first case the upper tent-like zone rises to an oculus, and in the second case a web of ribs, which has affinities with gothic design, spans the ceiling. The construction of Borromini's chapel at the Propaganda Fide involved demolishing Bernini's earlier chapel of 1634, located directly in front of the house and garden Bernini acquired in 1641 opposite the College. But before their falling out, in 1632 Bernini had recommended Borromini to Urban VIII for the post of architect to the University of Rome, the Sapienza. His first task there only came in 1642 when he was commissioned to design the church of Sant'Ivo in the limited space left unfinished by Giacomo della Porta, who had built the courtyard in the 1560s. Much of the church was built before Giovanni Battista Pamphilj (1574–1655) was elected Innocent X in September 1644, after which the project remained untouched until Borromini finally persuaded the pope to sponsor the construction of the spiral and lantern in 1651. Borromini's genius was once again demonstrated through his successive designs in which he altered and revised

204, 205. The remarkable interior of Borromini's Sant'Ivo (1640s–50s) comprises an undulating perimeter wall surmounted by an extraordinary cupola that rises to a small oculus.

the plans so as to derive the greatest possible space for the church, and then revised them again for his new patron in the 1650s. Notwithstanding the extraordinary combination of northern tribune, lantern and fantastic spire, nothing on the exterior prepares the visitor for the truly unusual interior. The plan of Sant'Ivo is clearly read in the entablature and comprises two interpenetrating equilateral triangles from which Borromini has, once again, subtracted so much that these generating geometrical forms seem to disappear: apses expand out from each side of one triangle and convex arcs eat into the tips of the other triangle, so that the six remaining straight segments of entablature are quite short in length, and dominated by the more powerful and larger apses and convex segments. Giant pilasters rise from floor level to the entablature, while ribs rise from entablature level to the central oculus which, together with the six large windows at the base of the cupola, provide the interior with abundant white light.

From 1644 onwards, through the influence of Virgilio Spada, who became the financial and architectural advisor to Innocent X, Borromini participated in papal projects such as the renovation led by Girolamo Rainaldi of the Pamphilj palace complex on Piazza Navona, where he designed the Gallery in 1646,

203
204
205

207. Sant'Agnese on Piazza Navona in Rome was begun in 1652 by Carlo Rainaldi, but was modified by Borromini and also Bernini.

and was involved for a time in the design and construction of the adjacent church of Sant'Agnese in Piazza Navona. In anticipation of the Jubilee year of 1650, from 1646 Borromini undertook the difficult task of renovating the basilica of San Giovanni in Laterano, the cathedral of Rome, without altering the original plan or the existing walls. He strategically recycled the green marble columns from the aisles and deployed them effectively for the grand niches that adorn the nave, being rewarded for his achievement with a knighthood by Innocent X in 1652. In addition to these public projects, Borromini also undertook private

208. Only the lower half of the façade of Borromini's San Carlo alle Quattro Fontane in Rome was built before his death. The upper half was altered in execution by Borromini's nephew Bernardo (1675–77).

commissions, including the renovation of palaces, for Orazio Falconieri in 1646–51, and for Virgilio Spada's brother Bernardino in 1650–53. Borromini designed a grand but unrealised palace for Ambrogio Carpegna in 1638, and after the death of the patron in 1643 he designed a much smaller palace for Ambrogio's brother Ulderico on the site adjacent to the Trevi Fountain. From 1653 onwards Borromini worked on the construction of another striking addition to the Roman skyline with the extraordinary travertine campanile to accompany the finely constructed brick tribune of San Andrea delle Fratte.

Towards the end of his career, Borromini returned to his early masterpiece to provide San Carlo with a façade, begun to a 202 new and more undulating design in 1665. In 1666 Borromini 208 obtained permission to build himself a burial chapel off the crypt, and by 1667 the façade had been completed to the main cornice. But the upper storey was only completed in 1675–77 by Borromini's nephew Bernardo (1643–1709), who had been married in San Carlo in October 1667 just three months after his uncle's death. Already in 1656–57 Borromini had become increasingly isolated both from his peers, including even his friend Pietro da Cortona, and his patrons including Virgilio Spada because of his refusal to proceed with work both at the Lateran and on the palazzo Spada; Borromini even absented himself for months from the Sant'Agnese project and was thus dismissed in early 1657. Spada died in 1662, and Borromini's only close friend after this time was the antiquarian and writer Fioravante Martinelli (1599–1667), with whom Borromini conceived and undertook the project of publishing the earlier manuscript on the Oratory that Spada and he had authored, together with engravings of his buildings. But Martinelli died on 27 July 1667 and, with the loss of the one person alive who profoundly knew and understood him, Borromini became deeply melancholic, burned some of his drawings, and finally, in the early morning of 2 August 1667, in his house on the Tiber at San Giovanni dei Fiorentini, he committed suicide by plunging a sword into himself, dying the next morning at dawn. He had changed the direction of European architecture.

Select Bibliography

General

Individual biographies of the architects discussed in this book may be found in the still unsurpassed *Macmillan Encyclopedia of Architects*, ed. A. Placzek, 4 vols., New York & London, 1982, and in the *Dictionary of Art*, ed. J. Turner, 34 vols., New York & London, 1996. The history of many individual cities can be found in the volumes of *La città nella storia d'Italia*, ed. C. De Seta, Rome & Bari, 1980 onwards, and the *Touring Club Italiano* volumes remain invaluable for their accounts of both the cities and regions of Italy. The history of the period is set out in E. Cochrane, *Italy 1530–1630*, London, 1988. The most important surveys of the period are D. Del Pesco, *L'architettura del seicento*, Turin, 1998, and the Electa History of Italian Architecture: A. Bruschi ed., *Il primo cinquecento*, Milan, 2002; C. Conforti and R. Tuttle eds., *Il secondo cinquecento*, Milan, 2001; A. Scotti ed., *Il seicento*, Milan, 2002. In English the standard accounts are R. Wittkower, *Art and Architecture in Italy 1600–1750*, rev. ed. J. Connors & J. Montagu, New Haven & London, 1999 (1st ed. 1958), and W. Lotz, *Architecture in Italy 1500 to 1600*, rev. ed. D. Howard, New Haven & London, 1995 (1st ed. 1974). Other significant works include the difficult account by M. Tafuri, *L'architettura del Manierismo del cinquecento europeo*, Rome, 1966, the brilliant account of all the arts by J. Shearman, *Mannerism*, London, 1967, and the collection of various essays G. Spagnesi ed.,

L'architettura a Roma e in Italia (1580–1621), 2 vols., Rome, 1989. L. Cheney ed., *Readings in Italian Mannerism*, New York, 1997, reprints the most important earlier essays. For patronage see M. Hollingsworth, *Patronage in Sixteenth Century Italy*, London, 1996, and for processions and temporary architecture see B. Wisch & S. Munshower, '*All the world's a stage...': Art and Pageantry in the Renaissance and Baroque*, Pennsylvania, 1990, and H. Millon & S. Munshower eds., *An Architectural Progress in the Renaissance and Baroque, Sojourns In and Out of Italy*, Pennsylvania, 1992. Important early studies include, H. Wöfflin, *Renaissance and Baroque*, trans. K. Simon, London, 1964 (1st German ed. 1888); A. Riegl, *Die Entstehung der Barockkunst in Rom*, Vienna, 1908; M. Briggs, *Baroque Architecture*, London, 1913; A. Venturi, *Architettura del Cinquecento* (Storia dell'Arte Italiana), 3 vols., Milan, 1938–40; R. Wittkower, *Gothic versus Classic*, London, 1974; Idem, *Studies in the Italian Baroque*, London, 1975. The most important journal remains the *Journal of the Society of Architectural Historians*, 1941 onwards.

Chapter One. Michelangelo and his contemporaries

1) MICHELANGELO. The best, very brief, account of Michelangelo's architecture is to be found in the relevant subsections written by Caroline Elam of the artist's entry in the *Dictionary of Art* (see above). The best overall account remains J. Ackerman, *The Architecture of Michelangelo*, rev.ed.,

Harmondsworth, 1986 (1st ed. 1960). Also see G.C. Argan and B. Contardi, *Michelangelo architetto*, Milan, 1990, and the fascinating study W. Wallace, *Michelangelo at S. Lorenzo*, Cambridge, 1994.

II) MICHELANGELO'S CONTEMPORARIES. E.H. Gombrich ed., *Giulio Romano*, Cambridge, 1999 is a collection of essays written on the occasion of an exhibition, as is C.L. Frommel et al., eds., *Raphael architetto*, Milan, 1984. Individual monographs include, E. Bartolini, *Giovanni da Udine, La Vita*, 2 vols., Udine, 1987; R. Cannatà & A. Giavarina, *Cola dell'Amatrice*, Florence, 1991; B. Adorni, *Alessio Tramello*, Milan, 1998; A. Pinelli & O. Rossi, *Genga architetto*, Rome, 1971.

III) NORTH–EASTERN ITALY. The intellectual context is set out in the exhibition catalogue L. Puppi ed., *Alvise Cornaro e il suo tempo*, Padua, 1980, and in the important account by M. Tafuri, *Venice and the Renaissance*, Cambridge Mass., 1989. Sanmicheli's varied work is discussed in the essays collected in H. Burns et al., eds., *Michele Sanmicheli: architettura, linguaggio e cultura artistica nel cinquecento*, Milan, 1995; P. Davies, *Sanmicheli*, forthcoming, Cambridge. An accessible account of Sansovino's work is by D. Howard, *Jacopo Sansovino: Architecture and Patronage in Renaissance Venice*, New Haven & London, 1987 (1st ed. 1975), whereas M. Morresi, *Jacopo Sansovino architetto*, Milan, 2000, presents an up-to-date catalogue

of his works. A good account of Palladio is presented in B. Boucher, *Andrea Palladio*, New York, 1994, while S. Frommel, *Sebastiano Serlio*, Cambridge, 2002 (Milan, 1998), mainly deals with his work in France.

IV) PAPAL ROME. Interesting aspects of the period are presented in M. Fagiolo ed., *Roma e l'antico nell'arte e nella cultura del cinquecento*, Rome, 1985. C. Frommel & N. Adams, *The Architectural Drawings of Antonio da Sangallo the Younger and his Circle*, Cambridge Mass., I, 1994, II, 2000, are extensive catalogues with introductory essays. R. Gaston ed., *Pirro Ligorio: Artist and Antiquarian*, Milan, 1988, is a collection of essays. For Vignola's work see the exhibition and catalogue by R. Tuttle ed., *Vignola*, Milan, 2002.

V) FLORENCE AND THE MEDICI. The best account of his architecture is C. Conforti, *Vasari architetto*, Milan, 1993, but for Vasari's life at court see L. Satkowski, *Giorgio Vasari: Architect and Courtier*, Princeton, 1994. M. Kiene, *Bartolomeo Ammannati*, Milan, 1995 is often inaccurate but has good photographs. See also A. Fara, *Bernardo Buontalenti*, Milan, 1995. Architectural designs of built and unbuilt projects are presented in A. Morrogh, *Disegni di architetti Fiorentini 1540–1640*, Florence, 1985.

VI) GENOA AND MILAN. The fundamental account of Genoa remains E. Poleggi, *Strada Nuova*,

Genova, 1968. W. Lotz ed., *Galeazzo Alessi e l'architettura del cinquecento*, Genoa, 1975 examines Alessi's work in Genoa and Milan. The best account of Pellegrino's work is R. Schofield & S. Della Torre, *Pellegrino Tibaldi architetto e il S. Fedele di Milano*, Como, 1994. The Milanese religious context is presented by J. Headly & J. Torriano eds., *San Carlo Borromeo*, Washington, 1988.

Chapter Two. Urbanism, building types, treatises

I) FORTIFICATIONS AND URBANISM. A history of urbanism in the sixteenth century is presented by E. Guidoni & A. Marino, *Storia dell'urbanistica. Il cinquecento*, Rome, 1982. Good accounts of fortifications are presented by H. de la Croix, *Military Considerations in City Planning: Fortifications*, New York, 1972, and J. Hale, *Renaissance Fortification: Art or Engineering*, London, 1977. M. Bevilacqua et al., *Roma Sisto Quinto: arte, architetture e città fra rinascimento e barocco*, Rome, 1992, examines the most 'urbanistic' pope, while the Jesuit order is examined in, T. Lucas ed., *Saint, Site and Sacred Strategy. Ignatius, Rome and Jesuit Urbanism*, Rome, 1990. The urban history of cities other than Rome include M. Fagiolo & M. L. Madonna, *Il teatro del Sole, la rifondazione di Palermo nel cinquecento e l'idea della città barocca*, Rome, 1981, and A. Scotti et al, *Sacri Monti*, Turin, 1991.

II) PUBLIC BUILDINGS. N. Pevsner, *A History of Building Types*, London, 1976, concentrates on the nineteeth century, but provides sketches of earlier development. Studies of specific building types include D. Calabi & P. Morachiello, *Rialto: le fabbriche e il ponte*, Turin, 1985; J. O'Gorman, *The Architecture of the Monastic Libraries in Italy, 1300–1600*, New York, 1962; L. Granshaw & R. Porter eds., *The Hospital in History*, London, 1989 and L. Magagnato, *Teatri italiani del cinquecento*, Venice, 1954.

III) CHURCHES. The most straightforward account remains A. Blunt, *Artistic Theory in Italy 1400–1600*, Oxford, 1940, and the best short historical account by N. Davidson, *The Counter-Reformation*, Oxford, 1987. Also see the case study by C. Robertson, '*Il Gran Cardinale*': *Alessandro Farnese, Patron of the Arts*, New Haven & London, 1992. For the Jesuit order see R. Wittkower & I. Jaffé eds. *Baroque Art: the Jesuit Contribution*, New York, 1972; R. Bösel, *Jesuitenarchitektur in Italien (1540–1773)*, I, 2 vols., Vienna, 1985; L. Patetta & S. Della Torre, *L'architettura della Compagnia di Gesù*, Genova 1992.

IV) PALACES. Most work has been on Roman palaces, notably C. Frommel, *Der Römische Palastbau der Hochrenaissance*, Tübingen, 1973. The social context is set out in K. Weil-Garris & J. D'Amico, *The Renaissance Cardinal's Ideal Palace: a Chapter from Cortesi's 'De Cardinaltu'*, Rome, 1980, and in the various essays collected in, J. Guillaume ed., *Architecture et vie sociale à la Renaissance*, Paris, 1994. The most brilliant account of palace design,

function and use remains P. Waddy, *Seventeenth Century Roman Palaces: Use and the Art of the Plan*, Cambridge Mass., 1990. P. Thornton, *The Italian Renaissance Interior 1400–1600*, London, 1991, is the only account of interiors, while various artists' houses are examined in E. Hüttinger, *Künstlerhäuser von der Renaissance bis zur Gegenwart*, Zurich, 1985.

V) VILLAS. D. Coffin, *The Villa in the Life of Renaissance Rome*, Princeton, 1980, remains the fundamental account, together with J. Ackerman, *The Villa: Form and Ideology of Country Houses*, London, 1990. M. Azzi Visentini, *La villa in Italia: quattrocento e cinquecento*, Milan, 1995, provides a thorough examination by region. For gardens see the excellent account by C. Lazzaro, *The Italian Renaissance Garden*, New Haven & London, 1990, and for the Rome region, D. Coffin, *Gardens and Gardening in Papal Rome*, Princeton, 1991. H. Bredekamp, *Bomarzo. Un principe artista ed anarchico*, Rome, 1989, examines this 'mannerist' park near Viterbo.

VI) TREATISES. There are three recent important accounts: J. Guillaume ed., *Les Traités d'Architecture de la Renaissance*, Paris, 1988; V. Hart ed., *Paper Palaces: the Rise of the Renaissance Architectural Treatise*, New Haven & London, 1998; A. Payne, *The Architectural Treatise in the Italian Renaissance*, Cambridge, 1999. Translations of treatises into English include: Vitruvius, *De Architectura*, trans. I. Rowland,

Cambridge, 1999; Serlio, *On Architecture*, V. Hart & P. Hicks eds., 2 vols., New Haven & London, 1996 & 2001; Palladio, *The Four Books of Architecture*, trans. R. Tavernor & R. Schofield, Cambridge Mass., 1997. Almost all significant sixteenth century treatises and architectural writings have been published with critical commentary in the important series by Edizioni il Polifilo, *Trattati di architettura*, Milan, 1966 onwards, and the same publisher has produced facsimiles of numerous other treatises. The best overview remains H.W. Kruft, *A History of Architectural Theory from Vitruvius to the Present*, New York, 1994.

Chapter Three. Scamozzi, Maderno and their contemporaries

I) VINCENZO SCAMOZZI. The only reliable account remains F. Barbieri, *Vincenzo Scamozzi*, Vicenza, 1952, as R. Franz, *Vincenzo Scamozzi: Der Nachfolger und Vollender Palladios*, Petersberg, Germany, 1999, is limited. For Vittoria see L. Finocchi Ghersi, *Alessandro Vittoria: architettura, scultura e decorazione nella Venezia del tardo rinascimento*, Udine, 1998.

II) THE SPANISH-RULED SOUTH. Apart from the writings of Daniela Del Pesco, the best account remains A. Blunt, *Neapolitan Baroque and Rococo Architecture*, London, 1975. A recent account is by F. Abbate, *Storia dell'arte nell'Italia meridionale: Il cinquecento*, Rome, 2001, but it has a limited

account of architecture.
For individual architects see
also the collection of essays, V.
Casale ed., *Cosimo Fanzago*,
L'Aquila, 1995; S. Savarese,
*Francesco Grimaldi e l'architettura
della controriforma a Napoli*, Rome,
1986; B. Laschke, *Fra Giovan
Angelo da Montorsoli*, Berlin, 1994.
For Lecce see M. Maniera Elia,
Barocco Leccese, Milan, 1989,
and for the intruiging architect
Del Duca, a start has been made
by F. Paoline, *Giacomo del Duca:
le opere Siciliane*, Messina, 1990.

III) THE ROME OF DELLA PORTA
AND MADERNO. The fundamental
account remains H. Hibbard,
*Carlo Maderno and Roman
Architecture 1580–1630*, London,
1970. Several overlooked
architects now have monographs:
L. Marcucci, *Francesco da Volterra:
un protagonista dell'architettura post-
tridentina*, Rome, 1991; M. Fagiolo
ed., *La Roma dei Longhi. Papi e
architetti tra manierismo e barocco*,
Rome 1982; B. Ringbeck,
*Giovanni Battista Soria: Architekt
Scipione Borgheses*, Münster, 1989.
Also on Borghese patronage see
A. Antinori, *Scipione Borghese
e l'architettura*, Rome, 1995;
Jack Freiberg, *The Lateran
in 1600: Christian Concord in
Counter-Reformation Rome*,
Cambridge, 1995; S. Ostrow,
*Art and Spirituality: the Sistine
and Pauline Chapels in S. Maria
Maggiore*, Cambridge, 1996.

IV) SOME DUCHIES AND THE
PAPAL STATES. For Medici festival
architecture see A. M. Nagler,
*Theater Festivals of the Medici,
1539–1637*, New Haven, 1964,
and J. Saslow, *The Medici Wedding

of 1589*, New Haven, 1996.
The account by C. Cresti,
*L'architettura dei seicento a
Firenze*, Florence 1990, is
inadequate. For the importance
of the Medicean Academy
see K. Barzman, *The Florentine
Academy and the Early Modern
State*, Cambridge, 2000. For
Farnese architectural patronage
in Parma and Piacenza see the
standard accounts by B. Adorni,
*L'architettura farnesiana a Parma
1545–1630*, Parma, 1974, and B.
Adorni, *L'architettura farnesiana
a Piacenza 1545–1600*, Parma,
1982; J. Southorn, *Power and
Display in the Seventeenth Century:
the Arts and their Patrons in Modena
and Ferrara*, Cambridge, 1988;
M. Bulgarelli et al eds., *Modena
1598: l'invenzione di una capitale*,
Milan, 1999.

V) NORTH-WESTERN ITALY.
On the important street see
C. Di Biase, *Strada Balbi
Genova*, Genoa, 1993; E. Gavazza,
Genova nell'eta barocca, Genoa,
1992; N. Carboneri, *Ascanio
Vitozzi: un architetto tra manierismo
e barocco*, Rome, 1966; A. Scotti,
*Ascanio Vitozzi: ingegnere ducale a
Torino*, Florence, 1969; A. Di
Raimondi & L. Müller Profumo,
*Bartolomeo Bianco e Genoa: la
controversa paternità dell'opera
architettonica tra 1500 e 1600*,
Genoa, 1982; G. Denti,
*Architettura a Milano tra
controriforma e barocco*,
Florence, 1988; P. Jones,
*Federico Borromeo: Art Patronage
and Reform in Seventeenth-Century
Milan*, Cambridge, 1993;
M. Pollak, *Turin 1564–1680*,
Chicago,1991.

VI) LONGHENA, CORTONA, BERNINI
AND BORROMINI: THE CREATION OF
THE BAROQUE. For Venice the
fundamental account remains
E. Bassi, *Architettura del sei e
settecento a Venezia*, Naples, 1962,
and the monograph on Longhena's
most important work by A.
Hopkins, *Santa Maria della Salute:
Architecture and Ceremony in Baroque
Venice*, Cambridge, 2000. An up-to-
date account of Bernini's
architecture is presented by
T. Marder, *Gianlorenzo Bernini
and the Art of Architecture*, New
York, 1999. Cortona's most
important work is thoroughly
examined by K. Noehles,
*La chiesa di SS. Luca e Martina
nell'opera di Pietro da Cortona*,
Rome, 1970. The essays in C.
Frommel & S. Schütze ed., *Pietro
da Cortona*, Milan, 1999, discuss
a vaiety of Cortona's works, and
A. Cerutti Fusco and M. Villani,
Pietro da Cortona architteto, Rome,
2002, is a complete and up-to date
monograph. On Borromini
see Anthony Blunt, *Borromini*,
London, 1979, and Paolo
Portoghesi, *Borromini*, English
translation London, 1968. Two
important exhibition catalogues
are M. Kahn-Rossi & M. Franciolli
eds., *Il giovane Borromini dagli
esordi a San Carlo alle Quattro
Fontane*, Milan, 1999, and R. Bösel
& C. Frommel eds., *Borromini e
l'universo barocco*, Milan, 2000.
A monograph by J. Connors
is promised.

Sources of Illustrations

Photo AKG London, Stefan Drechsel 164. Archivi Alinari, Florence 1, 3, 4, 5, 10, 18, 21, 22, 26, 28, 34, 44, 45, 46, 47, 50, 51, 52, 54, 61, 63, 77, 90, 92, 95, 107, 112, 114, 129, 141, 142, 144, 146, 148, 159, 165, 169, 170, 175, 183, 184, 200. Courtesy of the University of Birmingham Library 101. Osvaldo Böhm 31, 37, 190. British Architectural Library, RIBA London 14, 143. By permission of The British Library (from *Della Architettura Militare* by Francesco de'Marchi, 1599. Shelfmark 61.g.11) 70. Alessandra Chemollo 172. Courtauld Institute Galleries, Conway Library 15, 48, 55, 60, 133, 134, 162, 171, 177, 191. Electa Archive 187. Casa Buonarroti, Florence 6, 42. Uffizi, Gabinetto dei Disegni e delle Stampe, Florence 57, 91. A.F. Kersting 105, 207. Paolo Marton 140. Georgina Masson 9, 11, 27, 56, 59, 130, 174, 197, 203. Lala Meredith-Vula 24, 131. Biblioteca Ambrosiana, Milan 81. Fabbrica del Duomo, Milan 68. Archivio di San Barnaba, Milan 160. Melo Minnella 147, 149. Archivio di Stato, Naples 153. Photography Collection, Miriam and Ira D. Wallach Division of Art, Prints and Photographs, The New York Public Library, Astor, Lenox and Tilden Foundations 167. Fulvio Orsenigo 150. Ashmolean Museum, Oxford 20. The Bodleian Library, University of Oxford (from *Le due regole della prospettiva pratica, con I comentarij del r.p. E. Danti* by Giacomo Barozzi da Vignola, Rome 1583.

Shelfmark F6.15 Art, fol. 231. Plate XIII) 137. Archivio di Stato, Parma 113. Ente Provinciale Per Il Tourismo, Parma 176. © Luciano Pedicini/Archivio dell'Arte 84. Archivio Pubbli Aer Foto, Aerocentro Varesino, s.r.l. 82, 109, 121. Publifoto, Genoa 93. Biblioteca Vaticana, Rome 195. Gabinetto Fotografico Nazionale, Rome 96. Istituto Centrale per il Catalogo e la Documentazione, Rome 65, 157. G.E. Kidder Smith Collection, Courtesy of the Rotch Library Visual Collections, MIT 189. The Royal Collection © 2002, Her Majesty Queen Elizabeth II 193. Scala 192. Archivio Storico Comunale Torino, Colleziione Simeom (ASCT, Coll. Simeom, D 254) 179. Biblioteca Reale, Turin 155. C. Vajenti 39, 40, 86. Andrea Vicentino, *The Entry of Henry III into Venice*, 1574, Musei Civici Veneziani, Palazzo Ducale, Venice 75. Soprintendenza di Monumenti, Venice 117. Fototecnica, Venice 69. Vera Fotografia 71. Graphische Sammlung Albertina, Vienna 194, 196, 199, 202. Archivio Fotografico d'Arte A. Villani & Figli s.r.l. 80.

Index

DATE DUE